# THE ALT-RIGHT

## WHAT EVERYONE NEEDS TO KNOW®

D1252852

# THE ALT-RIGHT

## WHAT EVERYONE NEEDS TO KNOW®

## GEORGE HAWLEY

OXFORD

UNIVERSITY PRESS

# OXFORD
UNIVERSITY PRESS

Oxford University Press is a department of the University of Oxford. It furthers the University's objective of excellence in research, scholarship, and education by publishing worldwide. Oxford is a registered trade mark of Oxford University Press in the UK and certain other countries.

"What Everyone Needs to Know" is a registered trademark of Oxford University Press.

Published in the United States of America by Oxford University Press 198 Madison Avenue, New York, NY 10016, United States of America.

CIP data is on file at the Library of Congress
ISBN 978–0–19–090519–4 (hbk.)
ISBN 978–0–19–090520–0 (pbk.)

1 3 5 7 9 8 6 4 2

Paperback printed by Sheridan Books, Inc., United States of America
Hardback Printed by Bridgeport National Bindery, Inc., United States of America

# CONTENTS

## 5   The Alt-Right and the Internet — 106

## 6   The Alt-Right Offline — 129

# 7 The Alt-Right and Conservatism                                       150

1

# THE ALT-RIGHT

## WHAT EVERYONE NEEDS TO KNOW®

# INTRODUCTION

It is hard to write accurately about fast-changing social movements, especially secretive ones with mostly anonymous supporters. They can change quickly, and statements about them can transition from being perfectly accurate to woefully outdated with shocking speed. That has been my experience researching the far right in the United States. Counting this one, I have written three books on this subject in the last five years. The first of these, *Right-Wing Critics of American Conservatism*, which I drafted in 2014, was an overview of those right-wing movements that were never fully incorporated into mainstream conservatism. It covered many ideologies, but it did include a chapter on American white nationalism. It is notable that neither *Alt-Right* nor *Alternative Right* appeared at all in that book. This was not a mistake at the time. I had heard the term before, but in 2014, the label *Alt-Right* had largely fallen out of favor; the far right had mostly stopped using it. Things changed quickly, and in 2016, it was sufficiently newsworthy to warrant an entire book. My book on the subject, *Making Sense of the Alt-Right*, was published in 2017; it was quickly joined by a deluge of similar books by other authors.

Despite its recent release, *Making Sense of the Alt-Right* is also outdated in many ways. At the time I was writing, the Alt-Right was almost exclusively an online phenomenon. It was a mob of mostly anonymous trolls, pushing racist memes and silly frog cartoons. Many people were confused by the Alt-Right and unclear about what the movement was. Was it just a collection of nihilistic young men, attacking political correctness out of boredom? Was it a catchall term for Donald Trump's entire populist movement? Was it just a rebranding of racist groups like the Ku Klux Klan (KKK)? Was it a group of cultural libertarians, committed to free speech and opposed to social justice warriors? In 2017, much of that confusion was cleared up. As the Alt-Right moved off the Internet and into the real world, its ideology became more apparent.

Although the Alt-Right's strategies have evolved since the term was coined in 2008, one thing has remained consistent. White nationalism is the core ideology, even if not everyone who adopted the label realized it. This was one of the movement's strengths. The term *Alt-Right* was innocent enough that people who adopted the label could interact with people on other points of the political spectrum without being immediately shunned. It was also a weakness, however, as its ambiguous nature hindered its ability to promote a consistent ideology.

The Alt-Right made international headlines in August 2017, when the "Unite the Right" rally in Charlottesville, Virginia, resulted in the death of a counterprotester and an upcoming murder trial for an Alt-Right supporter who is accused of committing the act. The Alt-Right immediately gained a reputation as a violent movement, which it has yet to shake. People were concerned that this latest iteration of white nationalism might spawn a new generation of right-wing terrorist groups. This has not occurred yet, but vigilance remains necessary, as there are far-right groups threatening to make such a transition.

In this book, I seek to provide clarity about the Alt-Right. I will explain how the movement evolved over its short history. I will discuss its ideological antecedents, especially those racist extremist groups that made so many headlines in the late twentieth century, but eventually fell apart because of their own dysfunctional traits. I will show the ways that the Alt-Right differs from these earlier groups, but also note points of continuity. In addition, I will discuss the Alt-Right's other influences, including those ideologies not focused on race.

It is possible that this book also will go out of date quickly. I suspect that the Alt-Right is already declining as a political and cultural force. Having suffered many setbacks, it is now turning on itself. Within a short time, the extreme right may once again decide that the *Alt-Right* label has outlived its usefulness. Even if that occurs, however, it is important to understand the Alt-Right. Its most effective methods will undoubtedly be adopted again. Those who would combat such movements should understand why and how the Alt-Right was able to experience such explosive growth, even if it comes to exhibit the same pathologies that brought down its predecessors.

# 1

# WHAT IS THE ALT-RIGHT, AND WHERE DID IT COME FROM?

## What Is this Book's Purpose?

This book will provide some insights into the so-called Alt-Right, which is short for "alternative right." On its face, the term *Alt-Right* is innocuous, providing little information about the movement's ideological content. This was one of its strengths, allowing it to grow quickly in popularity. However, most observers are now aware that the Alt-Right is a far-right radical movement. Its mildest elements call for open and explicit white identity politics. Its most extreme voices are committed to white nationalism, ultimately seeking the creation of one or more racially pure white ethnostates in North America. The Alt-Right is not just a more racist version of American conservatism. The Alt-Right views all of politics through a racial lens, and it has little interest in political and policy questions that do not have an obvious racial angle.

The Alt-Right's motivating ideas are not new. Other movements, groups, and individuals have been embracing open white identity politics since the birth of the United States. The Alt-Right, however, is unique in that it is well adapted to the digital age. Although it is slowly trying to increase its presence in the real world, it remains a predominantly online phenomenon. Most of its supporters are anonymous. For most of its short history, online message boards, blogs, and social media were its main avenues for penetrating the public discourse. The Alt-Right engaged in relentless online trolling to promote racial discord and keep itself in the public spotlight. It used irony and humor to disarm opponents and maintain a degree of plausible deniability about its ultimate goals.

The term *Alt-Right* is about a decade old, but it first came to national prominence during the 2016 US presidential election, when the racial right was enthused by then-candidate Donald Trump's campaign. Although most members of the Alt-Right recognized that Trump did not ultimately share their core ideological convictions, his rhetoric on immigration helped push American politics in their direction. Important figures in the Trump campaign, most notably Steve Bannon (see the section "Are There Alt-Right Sympathizers in the Trump White House?" in chapter 8), who served as the Trump campaign's chief executive, briefly served as chief strategist in the Trump administration, and is the former executive chairman of *Breitbart News*, expressed sympathy for some Alt-Right positions.

The connection between President Trump and the Alt-Right is often overstated—the Alt-Right's ultimate goals are more radical and revolutionary than anything on Trump's policy agenda. However, Trump's presidential campaign energized the Alt-Right and helped the movement reach a new audience. Had Trump never entered the GOP presidential primaries, and had a more conventional Republican like Senator Marco Rubio or former Florida governor Jeb Bush been pitted against former secretary of state Hillary Clinton, the Alt-Right would not have shown much interest in the 2016 presidential election. The racial right's newfound interest in partisan politics was clearly due to Trump, even if his political platform differed from their own and Trump himself had little understanding of the Alt-Right.

The Alt-Right's growth seems to have stalled since Trump's ascension to the presidency. Whether it had any substantive effect on the outcome of the presidential election is debatable—the perceived connection between Trump and the Alt-Right may have cost him more votes than it gained. However, its direct influence on policy since that time seems negligible. A series of missteps throughout 2017 hindered the Alt-Right's outreach efforts. Its most significant real-world rallies and other public events were either duds or disasters. The Alt-Right's "Unite the Right" rally in Charlottesville, Virginia, in August 2017 ended with dozens of injuries and one death (see the section "What Was the 'Unite the Right' Rally?" in chapter 6). That event earned the Alt-Right a violent reputation, which it has yet to lose. The movement faces increasing difficulties spreading its message, both online and in the real world.

Unlike other right-wing ideologies such as conservatism and libertarianism, the Alt-Right does not offer a coherent or well-developed set of policy proposals. It has no major think tanks, and no elected politicians to date have publicly identified as being part of the Alt-Right. At this stage, the Alt-Right is focused on changing the ideological outlook of white Americans, pushing them to reject basic American values such as democracy and equality. It borrows the idea of "metapolitics" from the European New Right (see the section "Who Is Alain de Benoist, and What Is the European New Right?" in chapter 3). This concept, first developed by the Italian Marxist Antonio Gramsci, suggests that political power is downstream from cultural power, and no revolution will be ultimately successful unless a critical mass of the population accepts its fundamental premises.

Although there is no shortage of racism in white America, the number of people who support the Alt-Right's radical agenda remains small. Thus, the Alt-Right is presently more concerned with the viral spread of its ideology than with lobbying for marginal changes to federal policy. In the short term, the Alt-Right's promotion of racist Internet memes and slogans may be inconsequential. Over the long term, however, the Alt-Right hopes to expand the realm of acceptable political ideas, allowing an eventual breakthrough of open and explicit white identity politics.

Extreme profanity and the vilest racial, ethnic, and religious slurs are common within Alt-Right literature—although it is true that some elements of the Alt-Right eschew this kind of language. Vulgarity is an important element of the movement, as it relies on shock value to gain attention. Nonetheless, I will not quote any of that material within these pages. The ideas promoted by the Alt-Right are sufficiently alarming that I see no reason to bombard readers with repeated examples of vulgar and hateful language.

Although the Alt-Right's influence should not be overestimated, it is not going to disappear any time soon. It is now part of the public discussion. Even if the term *Alt-Right* falls out of favor, the sentiments that motivated the movement still will be shared by a nonnegligible percentage of the US population, and its more successful tactics will undoubtedly be used again by others. For that reason, its goals, supporters, and activities should be well understood.

This book is focused on the Alt-Right. However, to understand it, we must know what it is reacting against. For that reason, this book also discusses other right-wing movements, including mainstream conservatism, libertarianism, paleoconservatism, and earlier manifestations of white nationalism.

### What Is the Alt-Right?

Outside of any context, the only political information that the term *Alt-Right* conveys is that it is right of center and offers an alternative to the mainstream right. For a time, this was one of the term's strong points. As a vague phrase, anyone with right-wing inclinations who rejected mainstream conservatism might find it appealing. Over the course of its short history, the expansiveness of the label *Alt-Right* has waxed and waned. At its inception, it was an umbrella term containing people with several different ideological moorings—but this changed as it became increasingly associated with the radical right. It did not enjoy extraordinary growth during this period. Even the far right mostly abandoned the term by the end of 2013—including Richard Spencer, the person who coined it—but it came roaring back two years later on social media. In this subsequent iteration, it once again briefly experienced a moment of widespread appeal. It was used by people with multiple right-wing ideological dispositions until it again became explicitly and exclusively associated with white racial politics by the end of 2016.

White identity politics has been a central plank of the Alt-Right, even if some people who embraced the label thought otherwise. The Alt-Right views identity as the foundation of politics, and race as a key element of identity. It rejects the now-dominant notion that race is a social construct rather than a legitimate biological category, and it views the future success of whites as its predominant goal. The Alt-Right is additionally an anti-Semitic movement, and most of its leading voices consider Jewish influence on political life detrimental to whites.

Immigration is the Alt-Right's primary policy concern. It claims that immigration from the developing world represents an existential threat to majority-white countries. However, the leading voices of the Alt-Right want something more extreme than a reduction of immigration. The movement ultimately wants fewer nonwhites in the United States, even if that means the deportation of American citizens. Most of the major hubs of Alt-Right thought say little about how they would accomplish this. The Alt-Right typically avoids the exterminationist rhetoric employed by earlier white nationalists like William Pierce, author of *The Turner Diaries* (see the section "What Was The Order?" in chapter 2). Spencer, who created the term *Alt-Right* and remains the primary face of the movement, has called for "peaceful ethnic cleansing."[1]

Although hard demographic numbers are difficult to come by, the Alt-Right presents itself as a youthful movement. Most of its supporters appear to be white millennial men. They do not seem to be concentrated in any one geographic region; the Alt-Right can be found in the North and South, in rural, suburban, and urban areas, and in Red and Blue states.

## What Are the Core Principles of the Alt-Right?

Although the Alt-Right has many prominent figures, at this point it does not have a leader or group of leaders in the conventional political sense. Other ideologies possess a well-articulated manifesto or political theory that supporters rally behind. The early communists treated the words of Karl Marx as gospel. Postwar American conservatives mostly agreed with the principles articulated in the famous Sharon Statement, adopted by Young Americans for Freedom in 1960,[2] and Russell Kirk's "ten conservative principles."[3] The Port Huron Statement, which helped to unify the New Left, was adopted by Students for a Democratic Society in 1962.[4] For the time being, the Alt-Right lacks this kind of ideological consistency or unity.

Some figures associated with the Alt-Right have attempted to create a short list of principles that unite the movement. The blogger Vox Day, for example, has written "Sixteen Points" that he says define the Alt-Right.[5] Some of these points are widely agreed upon by those in the movement. For example, Day's claim that the Alt-Right is "anti-globalist" is uncontroversial among them. However, his definition excludes many people who we could classify as Alt-Right, and who use the label themselves. For instance, he claimed that "National Socialists are not Alt-Right," but the Alt-Right supporters who identify as neo-Nazis disagree. Those aspects of the Alt-Right that despise Christianity similarly reject Vox Day's insistence that Christianity is one of the "three foundational pillars" of Western civilization.

More recently, Richard Spencer attempted to lay out the unifying principles of the Alt-Right in what he called the

"Charlottesville Statement," published immediately before the "Unite the Right" rally. The statement opens with Spencer's catchphrase, "Race is real. Race matters. Race is the foundation of identity." The statement contained several common Alt-Right talking points about Jewish influence and globalization. However, the violence that occurred that same weekend overshadowed the statement's release, and the manifesto received little attention.

For the time being, *Alt-Right* includes anyone who identifies as part of the Alt-Right. The movement lacks the kind of organizational structure needed to enforce meaningful ideological conformity. The Alt-Right remains divided on many key issues, such as abortion, the role of religion in society (and which religious traditions should be favored), capitalism, and questions of tactics and strategy. However, although its members disagree on the policy implications of this stance, white identity is the Alt-Right's foundational principle.

Because race is the Alt-Right's most important issue, it necessarily rejects important elements of American political culture. Mainstream conservatives and liberals have long argued about the meaning of equality and what kind of equality they hope to achieve, but few contemporary conservatives openly reject it as a goal (see the section "Is Conservatism a Universalist Ideology?" in chapter 7). Conservatives tend to focus on the idea of "equality of opportunity," whereas progressives are more inclined to promote equality of material conditions. Conservatives and progressives also argue about which package of policies will ultimately lead to a more equitable society. Ideologues across the mainstream political spectrum argue about the correct interpretation of the US Constitution, the proper level of taxation, and how business should be regulated. The Alt-Right has little interest in those questions. White interests are the Alt-Right's main priority. If the Constitution, democracy, capitalism, or other elements of American political culture are inimical to white interests, then they would happily jettison them. For a thorough description of the Alt-Right's beliefs, I recommend Thomas Main's book, *The Rise of the Alt-Right.*

### Is Alt-Right Just Another Word for White Nationalism?

Yes and no. White nationalists were always the core of the Alt-Right, and white nationalists used the term as an outreach strategy. However, *Alt-Right* has not always been synonymous with white nationalism. Because it is an anodyne phrase, for a time some people who did not consider themselves white nationalists embraced it. This was especially true when it saw unprecedented growth in usage during 2015 and 2016, before most people understood what its leading voices really wanted. Some white nationalists have always disliked the label *Alt-Right,* rejecting the dissembling language and just calling themselves *white nationalists.* Others prefer the term *Identitarian* (see the section "What Is the Identitarian Movement?" in chapter 3).

Unlike white nationalism, which is an ideology, the *Alt-Right* label does not necessarily commit a person to a particular political philosophy. White nationalists used it because it helped them spread their ideology, and they will continue to use it if it remains valuable. The day may arrive when the term ceases to be useful. At that point, the radical right may drop it. This may already be happening, as many people on the far right—including some white nationalists—have abandoned the label. It is, therefore, worth noting that if *Alt-Right* disappears as a term, people who agree with its core principles will remain.

### What Is White Nationalism?

Racism and white supremacy have existed since the concept of race was invented. However, white nationalism is a relatively recent invention, only developing as we currently understand it after World War II. One thing that sets contemporary white nationalists apart from earlier racist movements is the degree to which they focus on whites in a broad sense. Earlier racist groups and movements in the United States were interested in the supposed differences among various European ethnic groups. For example, the racist eugenics movement was not just interested in the supposed inferiority of non-Europeans; it viewed many European groups with suspicion as well. The immigration restrictions of the 1920s were primarily a means of stopping the flow of southern and eastern Europeans into the United States (see the section "What Was the Progressive Movement of the Late Nineteenth and Early Twentieth Centuries?" in chapter 4).

Racist literature in the United States and abroad in the early twentieth century included lengthy discussions about the categorization of different European groups. Many of the policies in Hitler's Germany were based on the idea that Slavic peoples were an inferior race. Groups like the Ku Klux Klan (KKK) focused on religion as well as race, wanting the United States to remain both overwhelmingly white and Protestant and expressing hostility toward the nation's growing Catholic and Jewish populations.

Following World War II, white nationalism focused on whites as a larger group. White nationalists continued to debate who, exactly, qualified as "white." They still do so. However, today's American white nationalists generally agree that the category of white includes all non-Jewish people who can trace their heritage back to Europe. Part of this has to do with the demographic history of the United States. Although we should not overstate the degree to which the United States has ever truly lived up to its ideal of a "melting pot," by the mid-twentieth century, Americans labeled as white were increasingly likely to have multiple European ethnic groups in their family tree. The number of Americans who could describe themselves as 100 percent English or German or Norwegian was shrinking, and so they developed a new identity as generic white Americans.

Decolonization and the Western world's decline as the preeminent power on the globe also led white nationalists to promote the idea that global white solidarity was important. We can find earlier examples of proponents of white unity—Madison Grant and Lothrop Stoddard in the United States, Oswald Spengler in Germany. However, in the early twentieth century, most Americans and Europeans took it for granted that whites would maintain their dominant status in world affairs and that the United States and Europe would remain overwhelmingly white in the future.

Damon Berry provided a useful definition of the term *white nationalism*. He described it as "racial protectionism," predicated on the "belief that the white race is imperiled and that it is the duty of every white man and woman to do what they must to protect it from biological extinction."[6] This is the central idea of both the Alt-Right and its ideological predecessors.

### What Is Anti-Semitism?

*Anti-Semitism* means antipathy toward Jewish people. It is a very old prejudice. As the Anti-Defamation League (ADL) notes, "Hostility toward Jews dates to ancient times, perhaps to the beginning of Jewish history."[7] However, anti-Semitism can manifest itself in many ways and derive from many different justifications. In Europe after the rise of Christianity, hostility to Jews was often based on religion. Anti-Semitism is not always driven by religion per se, however. In medieval Europe, Jews were often barred from certain professions, or they took up professions that were forbidden for Christians. Moneylending was the most notable of these, as Christians at the time were not allowed to lend money with interest. The stereotype of Jewish "usurers" has persisted ever since and is a significant element of anti-Semitic propaganda.

Racist anti-Semites have also attacked Jews on the grounds that they are not a truly European people, despite their presence on the continent for thousands of years. A common argument among white nationalists is that Jews are a fundamentally foreign group and thus do not belong in white societies. The fact that they appear white, according to anti-Semites, actually makes them more dangerous because this makes it easier to forget that they are an alien people.

Although racism and anti-Semitism are correlated, not all racist and white nationalist groups have similar attitudes toward Jews. We can find examples of racists that are not particularly anti-Semitic. The Confederate States of America, for example, exhibited comparatively little open and official hostility toward Jews, as a few Jewish people held prominent positions in the Confederate government. Even today, several prominent white nationalists disavow anti-Semitism. Jared Taylor of the *American Renaissance* website and magazine (see the section "Who Is Jared Taylor, and What Is *American Renaissance?*" in chapter 2) is the most prominent of these.

Even though there are individual exceptions, the Alt-Right can be classified as an anti-Semitic movement. Alt-Right anti-Semitism is typically the result of ethnic rather than religious hostility. They consider Jews a separate "race," and one with interests that are inimical to whites. Kevin MacDonald, a retired psychology professor, influenced the Alt-Right's views on Jews. He has written several books purporting to show the negative influence that Jews have had on European societies in recent centuries, noting their disproportionate numbers in movements such as communism.

### Is the Alt-Right Misogynist?

Although gender is less central to the Alt-Right than race, we can describe the Alt-Right as a misogynistic movement, and most people who identify with the movement—including the women involved—would describe themselves as antifeminist. Different elements of the Alt-Right exhibit these attitudes to varying degrees, however. You can find voices in the Alt-Right with views on women that are similar to mainstream conservative views. They may prefer traditional gender roles but do not object to women being involved in politics. In fact, some people are eager to have more women publicly involved. By appearing friendly to women, the Alt-Right may appear less threatening and as a more normal element of American politics. Some of the most popular Alt-Right and Alt-Lite (see chapter 9) YouTube personalities are women, such as Tara McCarthy, Lauren Southern, and Brittany Pettibone.

But there is an element of the Alt-Right that genuinely despises women and wants them to have no part in politics. Reading Alt-Right material, one encounters arguments against women's suffrage. These people argue that women should not be allowed to vote because they are more likely to vote for left-wing ideas and less likely to exhibit extreme ethnocentrism. Others in the Alt-Right argue that women rob political movements of their cohesion and their presence leads to unnecessary drama. The worst misogyny can be found among those Alt-Right personalities pushing so-called white Sharia—the idea that women in the white ethnostate should have the same status as women in Saudi Arabia. *The Daily Stormer*, one of the most visited Alt-Right websites, was largely responsible for popularizing the concept.

Although there are exceptions, most of the Alt-Right does not demand traditional gender roles because they hold traditionalist religious views. Instead, the Alt-Right endorses what it calls "sex realism," which is analogous to "race realism" (see the section "What Is Race Realism?" in chapter 4). They argue that men and women have traditionally occupied different roles because they are biologically different. That is, men and women are hardwired for different tasks in society and the push for gender equality in all aspects of life goes against the grain of human nature. Instead, they argue that a traditionalist division of labor between the sexes—in which women are mostly focused on domestic tasks—is in the best interests of both men and women.

The Alt-Right's concern about gender relations is related to its obsession with race. Its proponents hate feminism and women's liberation in part because they blame it for declining white birthrates.

Although the so-called Men's Rights Movement (see the section "What Is the Men's Rights Movement?" in chapter 4) does not perfectly overlap with the Alt-Right, it shares many of the same ideas, and the Alt-Right has appropriated many arguments from Men's Rights activists.

### What Terms Does the Alt-Right Use to Describe Itself?

The Alt-Right's various factions have adopted different ideological labels. The Alt-Right's most radical elements have no problem describing themselves as neo-Nazis. This is not the modal view within the movement, though. Many people in the Alt-Right criticize those elements of the movement that embrace the slogans and aesthetic sensibilities of Hitler's Germany. These disagreements are often rooted in debates about persuasion; some in the Alt-Right view swastikas and other extreme imagery as bad propaganda, noting that these kinds of images alienate people who otherwise might be amenable to the Alt-Right's message. Others in the Alt-Right have genuine moral objections to the use of Nazi images and slogans.

Very few in the Alt-Right use the term *white supremacist* to describe themselves. They argue that the term is inaccurate because it implies an acceptance of racial diversity, provided that whites maintain a position of privilege. The term *white nationalist* is less controversial in these circles, as the desire for a white ethnostate is a common denominator within the movement.

Some in the Alt-Right have begun calling themselves "America nationalists." They avoid foreign symbols and slogans, and prefer to merge their racial views with the imagery of American patriotism. Those following this strategy argue that overt anti-Americanism, which is common within the extreme right, hinders recruitment. Thus, to reach American "normies" (see the section "What Is a Normie, and How Does the Alt-Right Apply the Term?" in chapter 5), they need to drape themselves in the flag and insist that their views on race are congruent with traditional American values.

Alt-Right supporters increasingly use the term *Identitarian* to describe their ideological orientation (see the section "What Is the Identitarian Movement?" in chapter 3). This is Richard Spencer's preferred label, and he seems to be predominantly responsible for the term's growing popularity in the United States. Like Alt-Right, *Identitarian* is not an inherently racial term. Although it implies a commitment to identity politics, it does not necessarily imply that race is the most important element of identity. However, Spencer and his followers regularly argue that race is the most important element of identity. The term *Identitarian* is a European import, and it had been used by right-wing European groups for many years before the Alt-Right concept was born in the United States.

### What Words Should the Rest of Us Use When Discussing the Alt-Right?

In 2016, there was a debate over the use of *Alt-Right* among mainstream journalists. Because the term itself provides almost no ideological content, discussing the Alt-Right without any context can mask the movement's racism and radicalism. The term's vagueness, furthermore, was clearly deliberate on the part of those in the movement. Unlike *white supremacist, white nationalist,* or *white separatist,* the term *Alt-Right* is not inherently threatening, nor is it even inherently racial, as already noted. Thus, people might be drawn into the Alt-Right's orbit without realizing that they are joining the ranks of a white nationalist movement. For this reason, journalists discussed whether they should even use the term *Alt-Right,* rather than simply refer to people in the movement as *white supremacists* or *white nationalists.*

However, if mainstream journalists and academics refuse to use the term at all, it becomes more difficult to explain the nature of the Alt-Right. The media's general solution has been to use the term *Alt-Right*, but provide additional context that explains the movement's ideological orientation. In late 2016, the Associated Press issued new guidelines about how the Alt-Right should be discussed. Whenever the term is used, according to these guidelines, the story should also clarify that the Alt-Right is "an offshoot of conservatism mixing racism, white nationalism, and populism," or, more simply, "a white nationalist movement."[8]

These guidelines may also be problematic, however, as they suggest that populism is an important element of the Alt-Right (see the section "How Populist Is the Alt-Right?" in chapter 4). Although the Alt-Right opposes contemporary Western elites, they are not opposed to elites as such. The populist position— which has both left-wing and right-wing varieties—implies that a virtuous "people" is being oppressed by a sinister "elite." The Alt-Right, however, is also generally contemptuous of most of American society. They do not simply loath the elites in media, politics, business, and academia. They are also critical of ordinary white people who do not share their views.

The extent to which the public is now aware of the Alt-Right's motives mitigates the problems associated with using the term. There was a time, particularly during the 2016 presidential election cycle, when *Alt-Right* seemed to encompass a much wider swath of the ideological spectrum, perhaps even being a catchall term for Donald Trump's right-wing populist movement. That no longer seems to be the case. Since the election, and especially since the 2017 "Unite the Right" rally, the term is now strongly connected with white nationalism. For this reason, there is less discomfort using it, although it remains important to provide context when it is discussed.

### If the Alt-Right Is Ultimately About Racism, Why Does This Book Discuss Many Nonracist Movements and Ideologies?

Few of the major voices in the Alt-Right have been lifelong, committed white nationalists. Most found their first ideological home elsewhere. Within the contemporary Alt-Right, we can find former supporters of positions across the political spectrum, including on the left. However, some ideological trajectories are more common than others, and there are obvious links between the Alt-Right and other varieties of right-wing thought, including some that are explicitly antiracist. Many Alt-Right personalities were once libertarians. Others came out of mainstream conservatism. There is a significant connection between the Alt-Right and paleoconservatism, though this is sometimes overstated.

When I make these connections, I am not arguing for guilt by association. The fact that many people entered the Alt-Right after passing through a conservative, libertarian, or paleoconservative phase does not prove that these other ideologies are invariably racist. In fact, many people in the Alt-Right who once identified with these other ideologies have contempt for their former political allies.

Nonetheless, there are elements of these other political philosophies that are ideologically proximate to the Alt-Right, and these ideas often served as a bridge between mainstream right-wing ideologies and radical white identity politics. These connections must be explored if we are to make sense of the Alt-Right.

### How Did the Alt-Right Begin?

The term *Alternative Right* (it was not generally shortened to *Alt-Right* until later) was first invented in 2008. The label was inspired by a speech given by the paleoconservative Paul Gottfried at an event hosted by his group, the HL Mencken Club. The speech itself did not call for the creation of a white nationalist movement. Instead, Gottfried simply noted that an alternative to the mainstream, predominantly neoconservative right was beginning to form.[9] This idea apparently inspired Richard Spencer, who coined the term *Alternative Right* and began to use it with some frequency at *Taki's Magazine*, which he edited at the time.

As mentioned previously, the term was not invariably racial at first. Gottfried himself did not indicate that this rising alternative right would focus on race; rather, he suggested that it would have a libertarian orientation. However, over time, as Spencer's racial views became more explicit, the racial aspects of the Alt-Right became more apparent, and it became predominantly associated with white identity politics.

### Who Is Richard Spencer?

It would be incorrect to describe Richard Spencer as the leader of the Alt-Right because such a description implies a greater level of organization and hierarchy within the movement than presently exists. He is, however, the Alt-Right's most well known figure. This is largely because he invented the term, but also because he was willing to be the movement's public face. The Alt-Right contains a large number of writers and podcasters who prefer to remain anonymous and always create content under pseudonyms. Some of the people in the Alt-Right whose identities are known today were exposed unwillingly. That is, they were doxed by their ideological enemies (see the section "What Is Doxing?" in chapter 10). Spencer has always expressed his views openly, although they have become more radical and explicit over the last decade. His willingness to speak with journalists has also contributed to his notoriety, as has his position as the president of the National Policy Institute (NPI), a white nationalist think tank (see the section "What Is the National Policy Institute?" in chapter 6).

Spencer was in a unique position to be the face of a radical movement because he was apparently born into considerable wealth.[10] Being associated publicly with white nationalism can cause financial ruin. During 2017, many people lost their jobs—including low-paying jobs with no ideological element—when their Alt-Right activities were exposed. This threat is a significant impediment to the Alt-Right. Due to his apparent financial security, however, Spencer has fewer disincentives to embrace radical politics openly.

Spencer first began writing about politics for a popular audience in 2007, when he contributed an article to *The American Conservative* focusing on the Duke lacrosse scandal, which involved several white students who were falsely accused of raping a black woman. At the time, Spencer was a PhD student at Duke. His previous education included an undergraduate degree from the University of Virginia and an MA from the University of Chicago. Shortly after the article's publication, he abandoned his academic aspirations and became an editor at *The American Conservative*.

Spencer was fired from *The American Conservative* a short time later. The exact reasons for his dismissal are not entirely clear, although ideological differences with the rest of the magazine's staff appear to have been a primary reason. In 2008, Spencer became the editor of a webzine called *Taki's Top Drawer* (later renamed *Taki's Magazine*), named after the site's creator, a paleoconservative named Taki Theodoracopulos. Spencer took over from the previous editor, F. J. Sarto. Before Spencer took the helm at that webzine, its contributors, while outside the mainstream of conservatism, were not particularly controversial. These writers included several well-known paleoconservatives and libertarians. Spencer soon began offering space to more controversial voices, such as the white nationalist Jared Taylor (see the section "Who Is Jared Taylor, and What Is *American Renaissance*?" in chapter 2).

As was the case with *The American Conservative*, Spencer's time at *Taki's Magazine* was relatively short. He left that position in late 2009. In 2010, he began a new venture, a website simply called *Alternative Right*. This did not focus exclusively on race; it also published a number of articles on culture, economics, and foreign policy. However, when it did venture into racial questions, it was much more explicitly racist than anything published at either *The American Conservative* or *Taki's Magazine*. Although Spencer was not publicly using the term *white nationalist* to describe himself or his website at the time, its content was pointing in a white nationalist direction.

Spencer once again switched his focus after a short time, giving up editorial control of *Alternative Right* in 2012 to focus on running the NPI and a new website and print journal called *Radix*. Although he is now known as the face of the Alt-Right, it was around this time that Spencer abandoned the term. The following year, he shut down *Alternative Right* entirely, apparently without first consulting its new editors.

Spencer continued to write, organize conferences, and give talks during this period, but he was no longer predominantly associated with the term *Alt-Right*. It was not until the term was revived by others, apparently without any direction from Spencer, that he once again became known as the face of the Alt-Right.

### How Did the Alt-Right Revive?

After Spencer shut down *Alternative Right*, the Alt-Right concept appeared to be finished. The former editors of *Alternative Right* created a new website shortly thereafter, using a free blogging platform, but its audience did not seem to be growing. In early 2015, however, the term experienced a significant revival on various message boards and on social media. White nationalists on Twitter began to use the hashtag #altright with increasing frequency. Aside from being vague, *Alt-Right* was a useful term because it is short. Twitter users at the time were limited to 140 characters (this has since increased to 280), so Alt-Right was helpful because it consumed comparatively few of them. The term became even more popular after Donald Trump's presidential campaign began, when white nationalists online made supporting Trump one of their most common activities. This revival was apparently spontaneous rather than due to any group's or individual's concerted efforts.

However, the term *Alt-Right* did not gain immediate popularity among all elements of the online radical right. Some people continued to avoid it. The term really took off in popularity when it began to be used by the popular media as a description of the new online white nationalist movement and the troll culture that promoted it (see the section "What Is a Troll?" in chapter 5). Once the term gained a high level of public notoriety, the far right mostly embraced it, including people who once had misgivings. It is now ubiquitous on white nationalist websites.

## How Large Is the Alt-Right?

Because the Alt-Right is a predominantly online, largely anonymous movement, estimating its size involves a lot of guesswork. Depending on what numbers one trusts and how one defines the Alt-Right, the movement's size ranges between the thousands to tens of millions. The high estimate is based on a 2017 poll conducted by ABC News and the *Washington Post*, in which 10 percent of respondents said that they support the Alt-Right.[11] If that number is correct, then there may be more than 20 million Alt-Right supporters.

There are strong reasons to be skeptical of that estimate, though. The "Unite the Right" rally in August 2017 was the largest Alt-Right event to date, and the largest gathering of white nationalists in more than a decade. Although it was a significant event for that reason alone, it is important to recall that it attracted only a few hundred attendees. Some of the organizers argued that the event would have been much larger, but because authorities shut it down before it even began, a number of people never reached the park where it was scheduled to take place. That said, even these organizers concede that the event would have drawn, at the absolute most, a little more than a thousand people. If the movement could really claim many millions of supporters, and if those supporters are distributed even somewhat evenly across the United States, there should have been tens of thousands of people within easy driving distance of Charlottesville that shared Alt-Right beliefs and would have been attracted by such an event.

Some may counter that the threat of doxing and exposure keeps many people who harbor Alt-Right sympathies from showing their faces in public, especially since expressing these views can get a person fired. This is almost certainly true. However, as the Alt-Right is predominantly an online phenomenon, it is difficult to imagine that many people seriously support the Alt-Right without also visiting the movement's main websites. For that reason, web traffic may be a reasonable proxy for the size of the population that is seriously engaged with Alt-Right ideas. Using this logic, Thomas J. Main of Baruch College sought to estimate the Alt-Right's size.[12] In his examination of unique visits, Main found that not a single website that could be properly classified as Alt-Right enjoyed more than 1 million readers over the course of any given month, although if the largest Alt-Right websites are combined, the total monthly traffic was approximately 4 million visitors.

Even these unique visitor counts may be misleading, however. Not everyone who visits an Alt-Right website supports Alt-Right ideas. Some people end up at those sites because of an unrelated Google search. Others may have deliberately looked for these sites simply to find out what they are about, but after reading an article or two, they concluded that the Alt-Right was not something they wanted to support. Some may actively oppose the Alt-Right but consume their material to keep tabs on what the movement's followers are saying and doing. And although there is surely a large number of people who read this material and genuinely enjoy it, many would never express a racist opinion in a public forum. At this point, there is no way to know what percentage of people that consume Alt-Right material are active in the movement, but we can be certain that it is less than 100 percent, and it is probably much less than that.

The Alt-Right, furthermore, is adept at making itself appear larger than it really is online. At many online forums and on social media, it is possible for one person to create multiple accounts. This allows a handful of people working together to appear as a large and menacing online mob. At the start of 2015, the Alt-Right was a tiny movement, but it created the impression that it was a growing force by relentlessly trolling a subset of journalists, celebrities, and activists. This spurred many stories about the Alt-Right in the mainstream press.

For now, the core supporters of the Alt-Right represent a small fraction of the total US population, but its members have successfully projected an image of themselves as a much larger movement through their adept use of social media and other online resources (see chapter 5). This does not mean that they have no influence over American culture and politics; their memes and slogans have penetrated public discourse and attracted massive amounts of attention worldwide. They were one of the major stories of the 2016 presidential election. At this point, however, it would be inaccurate to describe the Alt-Right as a movement that enjoys massive public support.

### What Does the Alt-Right Do?

Alt-Right activity takes many forms. Some Alt-Right organizing looks like traditional political activism. During 2017, for instance, the Alt-Right conducted several public rallies. Alt-Right groups hold fundraisers to support their fledgling institutions. A small number of Alt-Right-supporting attorneys engage in litigation. Most Alt-Right activity remains on the Internet, however. Alt-Right personalities create podcasts, videos, blog posts, and long articles. Alt-Right supporters share this material on social media. Both prominent Alt-Right personalities and their anonymous supporters engage in regular Internet trolling.

To date, the Alt-Right has mostly avoided other forms of mainstream political activism. The Alt-Right does not seriously engage with public policy. There is no Alt-Right equivalent of the Heritage Foundation or Cato Institute, writing white papers with the hope of shaping legislation. There are no significant Alt-Right political action committees (PACs) supporting candidates for elected office. In fact, to date, no political candidate with a reasonable chance of winning an important office has openly identified as part of the Alt-Right (see the section "Are There Alt-Right Politicians?" in chapter 6). The two most well known organizations associated with the Alt-Right, *American Renaissance* and the NPI (both of which existed before the term *Alt-Right* was coined), are focused on posting material on the Internet and hosting annual conferences.

Over time, the Alt-Right may evolve and become more professional and integrated into ordinary politics. For the time being, however, it remains a loose and disorganized movement, focused on injecting white nationalist ideas into general circulation.

### How Does the Alt-Right Recruit?

*Recruit* may not be the right word when discussing the Alt-Right. As it is mostly not a membership-based movement, it does not have a formal process in which new members are initiated. Other white supremacist groups have been organized as criminal gangs, as religious cults, or in a manner analogous to more mainstream political and cultural institutions. The number of Alt-Right organizations that are formalized to this degree is small. Groups like the Traditionalist Worker Party (TWP) and Identity Evropa have formal members and seek to build a real-world movement. The majority of the Alt-Right, however, remains predominantly online, and real-world meetups appear to be mostly informal and social.

Instead of drawing formal members in, most of the Alt-Right is more interested in pushing its ideas into the national conversation. It seeks to "red-pill" (see the section "What Is the *Red Pill?*" in chapter 5) the largest number of people possible on the issues that it cares about, hoping that eventually a critical mass will come to share the movement's views on biological racial differences, multiculturalism, anti-Semitism, and the desirability of a white ethnostate.

Although it wants to spread its message as widely as possible, at different points the Alt-Right has viewed some social groups as more persuadable than others. Most notably, the Alt-Right used the Trump campaign as an opportunity to start a conversation with Republican voters. However, the movement has not looked exclusively to the right when looking for potential supporters. In late 2016, there were discussions within Alt-Right venues about reaching out to disaffected Bernie Sanders supporters. In late 2017, the Alt-Right hoped to make inroads in the skeptic community—a movement that seeks to debunk pseudoscience and other claims that cannot be demonstrated via empirical examination. Some voices in the Alt-Right seek to promote their views on science and race within these networks.

The Alt-Right online does not systematically target specific individuals for recruitment. However, on various Alt-Right forums, one can find advice for persuading individuals within one's social network to accept the Alt-Right worldview.

Offline, the Alt-Right usually spreads propaganda with fliers. Groups like Identity Evropa (see the section "What Is Identity Evropa?" in chapter 6) regularly place small posters in public spaces that contain an Alt-Right message. They usually also include a uniform resource locator (URL) so that interested people can look them up online. These flier campaigns are especially common on college campuses, as the Alt-Right is specifically trying to reach out to young people.

### What Events Led People to Join the Alt-Right?

We should perhaps view the justifications that radical ideologues give for the beliefs with some skepticism. Such people may provide post hoc rationalizations for their opinions. Nonetheless, we find several common stories from Alt-Right supporters who have described their "red pill" experiences. Many people who identify with the Alt-Right have pointed to racial controversies that occurred during the Barack Obama administration as the cause of their radicalization.

In recent years, shootings of unarmed African Americans spurred new questions of racial bias and inequality in the United States. These shootings galvanized advocates for minority communities and led to the Black Lives Matter social movement. However, some white Americans witnessed these events and reached a different conclusion. The racist right argued that media coverage of these events proved that institutions in the United States were systematically biased against *whites*.

Some in the Alt-Right point to the George Zimmerman murder trial as a catalyst for their radicalization. Zimmerman, a Hispanic man, was tried for the 2012 killing of an African American teenager named Trayvon Martin. White police officer Darren Wilson's 2014 fatal shooting of Michael Brown, also an unarmed African American teenager, was another event that garnered much discussion on the far right.

The Alt-Right argued that the media covered these events in a biased and dishonest manner, deliberately demonizing the shooters and inaccurately describing what transpired. According to the Alt-Right, these shootings were completely justified, and journalists, activists, and politicians were using these events as an excuse to generate hatred against whites. They made this argument even though neither Zimmerman nor Wilson was found guilty.

Refugee crises also led to a new wave of white anxieties. In the spring and summer of 2014, a large number of refugees from Central America entered the United States, fleeing violence in their home countries. In 2015, Europe experienced a similar, larger wave of migrants fleeing violence and poverty in the Middle East and Africa. These images of mostly nonwhites entering the United States and Europe spurred fears about white countries being "overrun" by "invaders."

More broadly, the Alt-Right is reacting to the demographic changes occurring in the United States and other Western countries. The United States is on track to become a nation with no clear racial majority in a few decades. Several European countries are on a similar trajectory. Fear of their future as a minority is causing some whites to turn to racial identity politics.

Many people in the Alt-Right insist that they were not raised racist, that they did not inherit their views from their parents. They say that they developed their views on their own, largely from reading material on the Internet. In fact, the notion that the so-called baby boomers are naïve and contemptible racial egalitarians, and thus responsible for the demographic decline of white America, is now a meme within the Alt-Right.

### Do Alt-Right Supporters Have a Psychological Profile?

Because of the Alt-Right's anonymous nature, studying the movement's supporters in a systematic fashion remains difficult. However, some scholars are making this effort and providing some initial results. Patrick S. Forscher and Nour S. Kteily recently released a working paper in which they sought to provide a psychological profile of the Alt-Right.[13] This study included a sample of nearly five hundred Alt-Right supporters, and a comparable number of people who did not identify with the Alt-Right. The researchers were then able to compare the two groups.

The study showed a few ways in which Alt-Right supporters differed, on average, from other people. For example, respondents were asked questions designed to measure their Social Dominance Orientation (SDO), which measures a preference for social hierarchy and dominance over other groups. The survey also measured personality characteristics, notably the degree to which people exhibit so-called Dark Triad traits, which include narcissism, Machiavellianism, and psychopathy.

The results for Alt-Right supporters regarding SDO were as the researchers expected. The study found that the "alt-right sample reported high levels of social dominance orientation, strong support for collective action on behalf of White people, and strong opposition to collective action on behalf of Black people." They were similarly "willing to blatantly dehumanize both religious/national outgroups and political opposition groups, reported high levels of the motivations to express prejudice towards Black people, and reported high levels of harassing and offensive behavior."

The researchers did indicate, however, that there were two distinct types of Alt-Right supporters, which they labeled "supremacists" and "populists." The former exhibited more extremist tendencies and higher Dark Triad scores. The latter were less extreme and more likely to show concern about issues such as government corruption.

At the time of this writing, this working paper has not been published in a peer-reviewed journal. More work remains to be done on this subject.

# 2

# "WHITE NATIONALISM 1.0"

## THE MOVEMENT'S PREDECESSORS

### What Is White Nationalism 1.0?

*White Nationalism 1.0* is a derisive term coined by the Alt-Right to define its ideological predecessors. It refers to those white nationalist groups and individuals that were active in the late twentieth century and the first years of the twenty-first century. They use that term mockingly because these groups were ineffective. They had a deserved reputation for violence and had little to offer well-adjusted white Americans. These groups were known for their constant infighting, and their leaders attempted to attract cultlike followings. In some cases, these white nationalists formed literal religious cults.

The Alt-Right has attempted to distance itself from these forerunners, insisting that it represents something genuinely new, as opposed to a mere rebranding of the preexisting movement. To some degree, this is true. Although the Alt-Right has the same ultimate goals as earlier white nationalists, the movement developed independent of these previous manifestations of right-wing radicalism. Alt-Right material rarely refers to Ben Klassen, Richard Butler, Matthew Hale, or any of the other major figures of twentieth-century white nationalism.

Nonetheless, the gap between the Alt-Right and White Nationalism 1.0 is not as great as many in the Alt-Right would like to believe. The Alt-Right has faced major setbacks over the past year, and in the process, has begun exhibiting many of the same pathologies as its forbearers.

### How Were Racist Movements Traditionally Organized?

Since the modern white nationalist movement was born, it often organized itself in a manner analogous to other political movements. It sought to create formal, membership-based organizations and engage in real-world demonstrations. Although it typically did not have access to mainstream newsstands, it sought to distribute literature through its mailing lists and other means.

As the social stigma associated with open racism increased in the latter decades of the twentieth century, white nationalist recruiting efforts became increasingly difficult. It became harder to attract quality adherents, and the people who joined these groups often had limited social prospects, had addiction problems, or engaged in criminal behavior. Some of these groups would be better labeled as criminal organizations than political movements.

Older white nationalist groups often revolved around a charismatic leader, who built a cultlike following. Although some of these groups cooperated, they also engaged in regular in-fighting. There were frequent, high-profile disputes among various groups. Organized white nationalist groups, especially those that engaged in criminal activity, also faced a perennial problem of government infiltration.

### What Is the Ku Klux Klan?

The Ku Klux Klan (KKK) is the most notorious racist organization in the United States. A group of former Confederate officers established the group in the South during Reconstruction. Its most infamous leader was the Confederate general Nathan Bedford Forrest, who became the organization's "Grand Wizard." The organization was dedicated to restoring white supremacy in the defeated Southern states, often using the most brutal methods to deny African Americans the civil rights that they were promised by the constitutional amendments that followed the war. The federal government quickly and justifiably declared the KKK a terrorist organization, and it fell apart after just a few years.

However, the KKK experienced a major resurgence throughout the United States in the early twentieth century, largely due to the 1915 film *The Birth of a Nation*, which celebrated it. The new KKK maintained its previous hatred of African Americans but added Catholics and Jews to its list of enemies, and it continued to use violent tactics. The KKK became prominent outside the South, especially in the Midwest. This new iteration of the group also eventually collapsed, largely due to the 1925 murder conviction of D. C. Stephenson, one of its most important leaders at the time. The Klan again experienced a resurgence during the Civil Rights era, when it fought new federal efforts to ensure equal rights for African Americans, including the Voting Rights Act.

The KKK has existed continuously since that time, but it is now tiny, disorganized, and marginalized. Alt-Right supporters typically deride the KKK as at best ineffective, and at worst as being full of federal agents. The KKK does, however, still hold occasional rallies. For example, the month before the Alt-Right's "Unite the Right" rally in Charlottesville, Virginia, the KKK staged its own rally in that city, drawing a few dozen supporters. The KKK does not have a centralized leadership structure. Several small groups describe themselves as part of the KKK, but they are not unified in a single, hierarchical organization.

Despite its small size, the KKK remains the best-known hate group in the United States. Part of its notoriety is due to the influence that it once wielded in American life, especially in the 1920s. In that decade, the KKK held massive rallies, including in Washington, D.C., and included respected public figures in its ranks. The Klan also made a permanent mark on America's collective consciousness with its outlandish costumes, titles (like "Grand Dragon"), and acts of violence. The terrifying image of a hooded Klansman burning a cross remains what comes to mind when people think about organized racism in America.

### Who Was Francis Parker Yockey?

Francis Parker Yockey was among the most influential postwar white nationalists, though he had many critics within the movement. Whether the Alt-Right realizes it or not, Yockey developed many of its commonly expressed ideas. He considered himself the philosophical heir of the German historian Oswald Spengler. Yockey viewed his best-known work, *Imperium*, as a sequel to Spengler's celebrated book *The Decline of the West*. The German legal scholar Carl Schmitt was also an important influence on him.

Yockey, born in Chicago in 1917, had been involved with the radical right since the late 1930s. He earned a law degree and was briefly involved with the war crimes tribunals in Germany after World War II, though he was fired after a short time. He spent the rest of his life trying to revive fascist ideals. He created a group called the European Liberation Front that he hoped would successfully spread his vision. Yockey networked and organized in the United States, Europe, and even Central America and Middle Eastern countries. To travel and agitate around the world, Yockey used several false passports. He was eventually caught doing so and was arrested in 1960. Days later, he killed himself in prison by consuming cyanide.

Like contemporary white nationalists, Yockey tended to downplay the differences among European groups, rejecting the nationalism and intra-European hostilities that led to the world wars. His long-term goal was the creation of a vast new empire that would encompass all of Western Europe. He wished to see the result of World War II reversed. He viewed the period between 1940 and 1944, when most of Western Europe was under Nazi control, as a moment when most of the West was united, and he thought it was disastrous that it was defeated and occupied by "barbarians."[1]

Although he influenced white nationalists in the United States and abroad, Yockey held some views that make him different from most of the contemporary radical right. For example, he had idiosyncratic views on the nature of race. He rejected Darwin's theory of evolution and did not view race as merely a biological category, as most white nationalists do today. Instead, Yockey viewed race from a spiritual perspective, though he was a racist and an anti-Semite. He was also vehemently anti-American—so much so that he wanted the far right to work toward an alliance with the Soviet Union. In Yockey's view, the Soviet Union was communist in name only, and in fact behaved more like a traditional imperial power. Some racist agitators from that period, such as George Lincoln Rockwell, despised Yockey's work for these reasons. Yockey's most important American admirer was Willis Carto, who worked to popularize his writings after his death.

Despite his detractors on the far right, Yockey's vision of a global fascist movement that transcends national borders is now a common trope within the Alt-Right. Yockey's goal of building bridges between the far right in the United States and abroad is also shared by the contemporary far right. In addition, he was one of the first Americans to publicly deny that the Holocaust occurred—in *Imperium*, he stated that gas chambers were a myth. For an introduction to Yockey's life and work, I recommend Kevin Coogan's book *Dreamer of the Day: Francis Parker Yockey and the Postwar Fascist International*.

## Who Was George Lincoln Rockwell, and What Was the American Nazi Party?

The American Nazi Party was among the more extreme and flamboyant white nationalist organizations that formed in the twentieth century. The organization was founded in 1959 by George Lincoln Rockwell, and it garnered considerable attention during the Civil Rights era. Rockwell had previously served as an officer in the U.S. navy, and his followers continued to refer to him as "Commander Rockwell" for the rest of his life.

Like the later Alt-Right, Rockwell was able to draw attention to himself and his movement by embracing an outlandish, right-wing aesthetic sensibility. Rockwell and his supporters flew swastika flags, marched in brown shirts, carried weapons, and made Nazi salutes. The organization created a magazine called *The Stormtrooper*. It is worth noting that they did these things at a time when World War II was still a relatively recent memory for Americans. Rockwell also started using a corncob pipe, similar to Douglas MacArthur's—Rockwell was fond of MacArthur and supported him during his brief presidential bid. When discussing Jews and racial minorities, Rockwell employed the most abhorrent slurs and spread outlandish conspiracy theories about a Jewish and African American plot to destroy America.

Rockwell had political aspirations, seeking public office on a few occasions. He ran as a write-in candidate for president in 1964, earning a few hundred votes. A year later, he ran for governor of Virginia, earning approximately 1 percent of the vote. Despite his abysmal performance, Rockwell remained adamant that he would be president of the United States one day. It is impossible to know how Rockwell would have performed in a more serious presidential bid, however, as a former supporter murdered him in 1967. The American Nazi Party did not long outlive Rockwell, but it spawned similar organizations. William Pierce, one of Rockwell's associates, later formed the National Alliance (see the section "Who Was William Pierce, and What Is the National Alliance?" later in this chapter). The National Socialist Movement (NSM) (see the section "What Is the National Socialist Movement?" later in this chapter) also has roots in the American Nazi Party.

In practical terms, the American Nazi Party's influence on American life was negligible. At its peak, it enjoyed at most a few hundred supporters, and its truly dedicated followers numbered far fewer. Rockwell's public speeches and propaganda did not derail the Civil Rights Movement. However, Rockwell and his movement succeeded in drawing a huge amount of media attention. The famous author Alex Haley interviewed Rockwell in the pages of *Playboy Magazine*. Rockwell toured the nation giving speeches at college campuses. Like the Alt-Right today, the American Nazi Party could draw surprising attention to itself by being as brash, offensive, and extreme as possible. Rockwell's activism had a performative quality that made him irresistible to journalists looking for a good story. For a longer discussion of Rockwell's life and work, I recommend *American Fuehrer: George Lincoln Rockwell and the American Nazi Party*, by Frederick J. Simonelli.

### Who Was Revilo P. Oliver?

Many people associated with the radical right in the United States once had connections with the mainstream conservative movement. None, however, were as closely tied to conservative institutions as Revilo P. Oliver, who was a friend and colleague of many of the most important postwar conservatives. Oliver had a PhD in classics and was a professor at the University of Illinois. He counted important conservatives such as William F. Buckley, Jr., and Willmoore Kendall among his friends, and he helped found *National Review*, the flagship magazine of the conservative movement. He was also one of the founding members of the John Birch Society (JBS). During his time in the conservative movement, he contributed hundreds of articles to conservative publications.

Oliver, however, never really fit within the conservative movement. He loathed religion, and Christianity in particular. More important, he was a strong anti-Semite, which put him at odds with Buckley, who considered purging the mainstream right of anti-Semitism one of the most important elements of his career (see the section "What Has Been Conservatism's Response to Open Racism in Its Ranks?" in chapter 7). Although he was opposed to communism, Oliver thought that the conservative obsession with communism was misguided, as anticommunism was a distraction from the struggle against Jews, whom he considered a greater threat to Western civilization. He broke with conservatives entirely in the 1960s.

After abandoning conservatism, Oliver lost access to all popular publications. However, he did become a significant figure in the white nationalist movement. He collaborated with William Pierce, founder of the National Alliance. He also began working with extreme-right publications, such as *Liberty Bell* magazine, and published multiple books that lambasted conservatism, Christianity, and Jewish people. Oliver committed suicide in 1994.

Despite his prominence in the conservative movement during its formative years, mainstream conservatives rarely discuss Oliver. For example, he was not mentioned a single time in George Nash's comprehensive history of the movement, *The Conservative Intellectual Movement in America Since 1945*. This is curious, as conservatives are typically eager to highlight cases in which they drove open racists and anti-Semites from their ranks. The degree to which Oliver has been airbrushed from their history books thus seems like an anomaly. The difference may be that, in this instance, it was the anti-Semite that abandoned conservatives, not the other way around. The conservative movement cannot claim that this break represented a great moral victory on their part. Oliver's long relationship with the conservative movement and its most important leaders is thus only an embarrassment to conservatives.

### What Are Skinhead Gangs?

Skinhead culture is a European import to the United States. The skinhead culture originated in the United Kingdom in the

1960s. It was a predominantly working-class phenomenon, and its followers were best known for their shaved heads (hence their name), tattoos, and style of dress (bomber jackets and Dr. Martens boots, for example). It was also associated with musical genres, especially punk. Alienation from mainstream bourgeois society was a hallmark of all significant skinhead groups.

Skinheads first appeared in significant numbers in the United States in the late 1970s. Although skinheads have always been overwhelmingly white, not all skinhead groups are racist. When the movement began, it was mostly apolitical. As skinheads diverged into left-wing and right-wing factions, some were devoted to fighting racism. Those calling themselves Skinheads Against Racial Prejudice (SHARP) have engaged in violent confrontations with racist skinheads. The white supremacist element of the skinhead movement is better known, however.

Racist skinhead groups are notoriously violent and have been involved in numerous racist assaults and murders in the United States. Skinhead groups have also aligned themselves in the past with other white nationalist organizations, such as the KKK and the Church of the Creator (CoTC) (see the section "What Is the Church of the Creator?" later in this chapter). Although they are in decline, racist skinhead gangs remain part of American life. According to the Southern Poverty Law Center, there were 78 active racist skinhead groups in 2016, down from the 2012 peak of 138.[2]

The Alt-Right is mostly disconnected from the racist skinhead movement, though there may be some skinheads that identify as Alt-Right. Skinheads are rarely mentioned on the major Alt-Right platforms, and the Alt-Right has a different aesthetic sensibility. Whereas skinheads emphasize their working-class origin and display it in their clothing, much of the Alt-Right prefers to appear more modern and polished, preferring polo shirts and suits to steel-toed boots and shaved heads. Whereas skinheads revel in their fierce and threatening appearance, the Alt-Right has sought to appear reasonable and well adjusted.

## Who Is Tom Metzger?

Tom Metzger was one of the most significant white nationalist organizers of the late twentieth century. During the 1970s, he held a leadership role in the KKK and served as a minister for a Christian Identity church (see the section "What Is the Christian Identity Movement?" later in this chapter), though he later abandoned the Identity movement. Metzger unsuccessfully pursued elected office on multiple occasions. Unlike David Duke (see the section "Who Is David Duke?" later in this chapter), Metzger always ran as a Democrat. On questions unrelated to race, Metzger often supported left-wing policy positions. Although he had once been a fervent anticommunist and member of the JBS, he later turned against capitalism and embraced the Third Position ideology, which he thought would make his views more appealing to economically disadvantaged whites.

Metzger's first foray into electoral politics occurred in 1978, when he unsuccessfully ran for San Diego County supervisor. Two years later, he won the Democratic primary election for the local congressional seat. Because of his racial views, the state Democratic Party disavowed Metzger, and he lost badly in the general election—which likely would have occurred even if the party had supported him, as it was a heavily Republican district. He made one final attempt to gain political power in 1982, when he pursued the Democratic Party nomination for U.S. Senate. He lost this race badly as well, earning a little under 3 percent of the vote.

After abandoning electoral politics, Metzger again focused his attention on organizing racist groups. He created the White Aryan Resistance (WAR) in 1983. WAR was particularly interested in recruiting skinheads. It was also responsible for multiple acts of extreme violence. In 1988, a skinhead group affiliated with Metzger murdered an Ethiopian immigrant. Although Metzger was not directly involved in the killing, a jury in a civil trial concluded that he was liable for inciting the act, and Metzger and his organization were ordered to pay millions of dollars to the victim's family. Because of WAR's lack of resources, this verdict was a serious blow to the organization.

Metzger is notable for his enthusiastic embrace of new forms of media. In the 1980s he ran a public-access television program called *Race and Reason*. He and his son famously appeared on *Geraldo*, the syndicated talk show hosted by Geraldo Rivera, leading to a melee in which Rivera's nose was broken. WAR also published a monthly newspaper. In addition, Metzger was an early proponent of using the Internet to organize racist groups and spread the white nationalist message. He created a website in the mid-1990s and later hosted an online radio show. Today, podcasts are one of the Alt-Right's most important propaganda tools.

### Who Was William Pierce, and What Is the National Alliance?

William Pierce, who was previously associated with the American Nazi Party and worked with George Lincoln Rockwell, founded the National Alliance in 1974. Before turning to racist activism, Pierce was a physicist who earned his PhD from the University of Colorado and later taught at the University of Oregon. Before joining explicitly racist groups, he was a member of the conservative JBS. The National Alliance board included the former conservative Revilo P. Oliver. Pierce eventually located the National Alliance headquarters in West Virginia.

From the 1970s until Pierce's death in 2002, the National Alliance was one of the most notorious hate groups in America. At its peak, it may have had as many as two thousand members, as well as chapters in other countries. A significant number of National Alliance members have been convicted of racist crimes.

Pierce used his platform at the National Alliance to promote extreme racism, as well as a philosophy that he called "Cosmotheism." Like many twentieth-century white nationalists, Pierce felt it important to provide a religious foundation for his political beliefs. Cosmotheism is a variety of pantheism. Cosmotheists do not believe in a personal god or gods and do not believe in an afterlife. Instead, Cosmotheists try to find meaning by protecting and improving the white race.

Pierce was also interested in using popular culture to spread his ideas. In the late 1990s, he purchased the White Power record label Resistance Records, which released racist punk and heavy metal albums. Resistance Records also released a computer game called *Ethnic Cleansing*, a first-person-shooter game in which the player murders minorities.

Pierce died of cancer in 2002. The National Alliance fell into disarray shortly thereafter. His successors lacked his charisma and organizational skills. Within a few years, the National Alliance ceased to be one of the more important hate groups in the United States. The group still exists and operates a website, but there appears to be little overlap between it and the Alt-Right, and few current Alt-Right supporters cite Pierce as an inspiration.

### What Was The Turner Diaries?

*The Turner Diaries* was a work of fiction written by Pierce, who initially published the book under the pen name "Andrew MacDonald." It first appeared as a series of short stories published in the National Alliance's publication *Attack!* The organization assembled these disparate stories and published them as a novel in 1978. It remains one of the most notorious works of white nationalist fiction ever written. The book traces the exploits of its protagonist, Earl Turner, as he engages in a race war.

The book is gruesome. The main characters slaughter blacks, Jews, and anyone affiliated with "the System." The book also describes the mass murder of whites considered traitors to their race on the "Day of the Ropes." It ends with the protagonist's final journal entry, written shortly before he flies a plane carrying a nuclear bomb into the Pentagon.

In the epilogue, *The Turner Diaries* explains how the victorious white supremacists have engaged in the systematic murder, via weapons of mass destruction, of all nonwhites across the globe. Beyond its obscene violence, the book is notorious because it inspired a few real-world terrorist attacks. The white nationalist criminal group The Order took its name from the secretive inner circle that directed the genocidal campaign in *The Turner Diaries*.

*The Turner Diaries* received even more media attention when it was revealed that Timothy McVeigh, who conducted the deadly bombing of a federal building in Oklahoma City, used ideas from the book. The terrorists in the novel built bombs using fertilizer when they lacked access to more conventional explosives. McVeigh did the same. Pierce denied any responsibility for the attack, however, noting that his book was a work of fiction and not intended to be a guidebook.[3]

### What Was The Order?

The Order, also known as "the Silent Brotherhood," was a terrorist organization that operated in the 1980s. As previously noted, it was explicitly inspired by *The Turner Diaries*, taking its name from the cultlike inner circle in the book. Robert Matthews, who was also a member of the National Alliance, founded The Order in 1983 in order to wage a guerrilla war against the "Zionist Occupied Government" (see the section "What Does *ZOG* Mean?" later in this chapter). The small group committed a series of armed robberies and developed a counterfeiting operation. It stole millions of dollars, much of which it subsequently gave to other racist organizations. A significant portion of that money was never recovered.[4] The group also murdered Alan Berg, a liberal Jewish radio host, and planned to assassinate Morris Dees, who founded the Southern Poverty Law Center, which monitors hate groups.

The Order was brought down in 1984, when the Federal Bureau of Investigation (FBI) traced Matthews to his home on Whidbey Island in Washington State. Matthews was killed in a subsequent shootout. Other members of The Order were subsequently arrested and imprisoned. Aside from Matthews, David Lane was the most notorious member of The Order. Lane is best known for coining the "Fourteen Words" (see the section "What Does 1488 Mean?" later in this chapter). For his role in The Order's criminal activities, Lane was sentenced to 190 years in prison. While incarcerated, he continued to write white nationalist material. He died in 2007.

### What Is the Militia Movement?

Militias are private paramilitary organizations. The militia movement is often conflated with white supremacy, and for that reason deserves some discussion in this chapter. However, the militia movement that briefly thrived in the 1990s was not predominantly focused on race. This is not to say that no militias were racists, or that white racial anxieties had nothing to do with the movement's growth, but most militias subscribed to a nonracial, antigovernment ideology, often combined with conspiracy theories.

Posse Comitatus was an early manifestation of the militia movement. It was racist and closely tied to the Christian Identity movement (see the section "What Is the Christian Identity Movement?" later in this chapter). This group was responsible for several serious crimes. Most notably, a Posse member named Gordon Kahl killed two federal marshals in 1983 and was later killed in a shootout. Posse members were also responsible for many smaller crimes, such as tax evasion. Because many militias do not recognize the U.S. government's legitimacy, they refuse to comply with tax laws and other regulations. Many militia groups expressed anti-Semitic conspiracy theories analogous to those expressed by white nationalists.

The militia movement has a long history, but it experienced significant growth in the early 1990s, when several shocking events convinced some Americans that the U.S. government was becoming tyrannical. In 1992, a standoff between federal agents and Randy Weaver and his family left three people dead near Ruby Ridge, Idaho. Subsequent trials determined that government agencies had behaved improperly, and the remaining members of the Weaver family were awarded massive financial compensation. The government siege of the Branch Davidian compound near Waco, Texas, was even more significant. The Branch Davidians were a fringe religious group. In 1993, a standoff between the group and federal agents ended with the deaths of eighty-two Davidians. These events were a major recruitment tool for militias, which enjoyed steady increases in their membership afterward. These groups often recruited at gun shows.

But the militia movement's growth came to a dramatic end in 1995, when Timothy McVeigh blew up a federal building in Oklahoma City, killing 168 people. McVeigh had ties to militia groups, and he claimed that his actions were a response to Ruby Ridge and Waco. The bombing was a devastating blow to the movement. Whatever goodwill it had earned because of recent government overreach immediately collapsed, and many organizations simply disbanded.

In subsequent years, groups endorsing similar ideologies emerged. Many of these newer groups, such as the Oath Keepers and the Three Percenters, have emphasized that they are *not* motivated by racism or anti-Semitism.

The Alt-Right has shown little interest in the militia movement, though there have been some connections. Several militia groups were present at the "Unite the Right" rally. These groups wore military-style uniforms and carried weapons at the event. They all claimed that they had attended to support the First Amendment rights of the rallygoers, rather than to express support for the rally's message.

For a better understanding of the militia movement, I recommend *To Shake Their Guns in the Tyrant's Face*, by Robert H. Churchill, and *American Extremism*, by Darren Mulloy.

### What Does 1488 Mean?

White nationalists have used the term *1488* for decades. It has also been embraced by much of the Alt-Right, though some of them seem to use it as an inside joke rather than a call to arms. It often appears in Twitter and on white nationalist message boards. These numbers represent a combination of two white nationalist slogans. The *14* represents the "Fourteen Words," first coined by David Lane. The Fourteen Words are "We must secure the existence of our people and a future for white children." This slogan was embraced by the white nationalist movement and is commonly expressed by the contemporary Alt-Right. The *88* is a code for "Heil Hitler" (*H* is the eighth letter of the alphabet). Among white nationalists on the Internet, *1488* may be the most popular slogan.

### What Is the National Socialist Movement?

After the American Nazi Party collapsed, its former members created multiple groups. The most famous and influential was William Pierce's National Alliance, but the NSM is another such group. The NSM was founded in 1974. At that time, it was called the National Socialist American Workers Freedom Movement. It did not adopt the shorter name until 1994, when a neo-Nazi named Jeff Shoep took over the organization.

Unlike many other contemporary white nationalist groups, the NSM openly adopted Nazi symbols. At public events, its members have historically worn Nazi uniforms and swastika armbands. The group enjoyed a period of robust growth in the early 2000s, when competing organizations like Aryan Nations, the Church of the Creator, and the National Alliance collapsed. As recently as 2011, it was described by *The New York Times* as the "largest supremacist group," and it apparently had hundreds of members.[5] The NSM website says that it has groups in dozens of U.S. states and multiple countries overseas. The true size of the NSM at any given time is difficult to estimate with confidence, however, and it is worth noting that it has never staged a public event in which hundreds of members appeared.

The NSM is best known for its public demonstrations. Although it has not altered its message, the group attempted to rebrand itself in 2016 by ceasing to use swastikas.[6] Since that time, it has increasingly cooperated with other groups, notably the Traditionalist Worker Party (TWP) and other groups associated with the new confederation of organizations called the Nationalist Front. The NSM was present at several significant white nationalist rallies in recent years, such as a "White Lives Matter" rally in Shelbyville, Tennessee, and the "Unite the Right" rally in Charlottesville.

### What Is the Christian Identity Movement?

The Christian Identity movement was once a popular religion among racists in the United States. The religion maintained many unusual theological stances. Most notably, it sought to reinterpret the Bible in such a way that white Europeans, rather than the Jews, represented the true "chosen people." The religion's roots can be traced to nineteenth-century Britain, where a small number of people argued that modern Europeans were direct descendants of the ancient Israelites described in the Old Testament—a movement called British Israelism. This belief never gained more than a small number of adherents at the time. The original proponents of the idea were not apparently motivated by racial, ethnic, or religious animus.

In the United States in the twentieth century, these religious ideas were used to justify preexisting anti-Semitism. Those who embraced these views concluded that Jews were a cursed race, and that nonwhites more generally possessed no souls. No mainstream Christian denomination has ever endorsed these theological positions, and few Christians have embraced them. Nonetheless, these ideas gained a large amount of attention after they were adopted by prominent American racists. Richard Butler of Aryan Nations, for example, preached Christian Identity ideas, and George Lincoln Rockwell of the American Nazi Party also endorsed Christian Identity.

Christian Identity has experienced a steep decline in recent decades. During the 1990s, it was an important faction within the broader white nationalist movement. Today, it has very little influence. Within the Alt-Right, there are numerous people who identify as Christians, but few who embrace the Christian Identity theology. The most popular Alt-Right websites rarely mention Christian Identity. For a useful introduction to the Christian Identity movement's history, I recommend Michael Barkun's book, *Religion and the Racist Right: The Origins of the Christian Identity Movement*.

### What Was Aryan Nations?

At the peak of its influence, Aryan Nations was among the more significant hate groups in the United States. Richard Butler founded the group in the 1970s. Butler, a former aeronautical engineer and inventor, hoped that the Pacific Northwest could one day become a "white homeland," and he built a compound for the organization in Idaho, near the tourist city of Coeur d'Alene. Like many white supremacist leaders of this period, Butler followed the Christian Identity movement. The Aryan Nations compound eventually became a gathering place for white supremacists. Butler held regular meetings that he called the "Aryan Nations World

Congress." The compound also hosted annual skinhead gatherings.

Butler and Aryan Nations were often closely connected with violent extremism. Robert Matthews and other members of The Order had connections with Aryan Nations. The Order gave some of the money that it stole during its crime spree to Butler, but law enforcement could not prove that Butler knew the money was obtained illegally.

Aryan Nations did not limit its activities to its own compound, hosting parades and flier campaigns throughout the community. Other locals objected to this, as they did not want their region to develop a reputation as a haven for white supremacists, but they could do little about it without violating the group's First Amendment rights.

A lawsuit brought down Aryan Nations in 2000. After Aryan Nations members assaulted two people outside the compound, the Southern Poverty Law Center filed a lawsuit on the victims' behalf. To pay the multimillion-dollar judgment that resulted, Aryan Nations was forced to sell its property. Butler died in 2004, and the organization split apart shortly thereafter. None of its offshoots have attained a similar level of national prominence, however.

Contemporary Alt-Right material rarely references Butler or Aryan Nations. Nor have any significant figures within the Alt-Right thus far followed the compound model of organizing, though the TWP (see the section "Who Is Matthew Heimbach, and What Was the Traditionalist Worker Party?" in chapter 6) apparently owned property where multiple members resided. However, Butler's ideas about the Pacific Northwest as the ideal place for a new white homeland are still promoted by some white nationalists.

### What Is the Northwest Front?

The Northwest Front wants to create a new white nation in the Pacific Northwest, hoping to spark a racist separatist movement in Washington, Oregon, Idaho, and western Montana. Richard Butler of Aryan Nations is best known for popularizing the idea, though he was inspired by a former KKK leader named Robert Miles. Harold Covington, who has been involved with white nationalist causes since the early 1970s, is now the person most associated with this idea. Covington has a long history of feuding with other white nationalists; Ben Klassen and William Pierce, for example, disparaged him.

Like Pierce, Covington has laid out his vision in a series of novels. He has written four novels explaining how a guerrilla war by white nationalists could cause racial minorities and the U.S. federal government to flee the region. He argues that a persistent, violent campaign, using tactics developed by the Irish Republican Army (IRA) to fight British control of Northern Ireland, could eventually make it impossible to govern the region.

As was the case with Pierce, Covington insists that his works of fiction are not intended to inspire any acts of real-world violence. But Covington was one of the few people explicitly named in Dylann Roof's manifesto, which came to light at the time of his murderous rampage in Charleston, South Carolina. For now, however, Covington's main activism is focused on encouraging white nationalists to move to the Northwest and form communities of like-minded people.

Covington continues to fight with other white nationalists, and contemporary Alt-Right platforms only infrequently cite Covington as a model. The idea that some portion of the United States should be carved out as a homeland for whites has been a common theme in white nationalist literature, however. Tom Metzger has drawn a similar (though larger) map of what he called the "White American Bastion." Contemporary Southern nationalists would like to see the original Confederate States of America re-created (see the section "What Is the Neo-Confederate Movement?" later in this chapter).

## What Is the Church of the Creator?

The CoTC, also known as the Creativity Movement, is a religious group created by Ben Klassen in 1973, though we must apply the term *religion* somewhat loosely in this context. Klassen and his followers did not believe in anything supernatural. In fact, they rejected all religious claims about gods and the afterlife. Instead, they wanted whites to pursue the improvement and expansion of their race with the zeal of religious fanatics.

Before turning all his attention to racist activism, Klassen was involved in conventional politics. He was a member of the JBS and briefly served as a representative in the Florida legislature. Klassen rejected all religions, but he despised Christianity in particular because of its effects on the white race. He argued that Christianity was actually a Jewish conspiracy designed to enslave whites, and that its maxims about forgiveness and celebrations of weakness were detrimental to whites. His contempt for Christianity was so strong that he even rejected the racialized versions of Christianity that were popular among some white nationalists during his time—he had no patience with Christian Identity, for example.

In place of Christianity, Klassen wanted a religion built explicitly and entirely around race, devoid of any references to the supernatural. He wrote three "holy books" that would serve as the foundation for Creativity: *Nature's Eternal Religion*, *The White Man's Bible*, and *Salubrious Living*. Although Klassen did not believe in any supernatural intelligence, he argued that "nature" provided certain lessons that humankind must absorb in order to thrive. These ideas were intuitive to Klassen, but he felt that Christianity and liberal ideologies had blinded whites to their truth. According to Klassen, every species and subspecies has a natural drive to strengthen itself and expand as widely as possible. He thus made this the central aim of his religion. In fact, the religion holds that anything that benefits the white race represents "the highest good." Klassen gave himself the title "Pontifex Maximus." He had great aspirations for his organization and hoped that his compound would eventually be a training ground for the next generation of white nationalists. He wanted to create a "school for gifted boys," where young boys would be indoctrinated into his belief system and prepared for a lifetime of activism and leadership.

Creativity enjoyed meaningful growth during the 1980s, but like other racist organizations of that period, it was hamstrung by its own violence. A Creativity leader was convicted of murdering an African American man in 1991, and the CoTC was eventually forced to pay a $1 million settlement to the victim's family. In 1993, law enforcement thwarted several violent plots by Creativity followers. Klassen killed himself that same year.

Creativity enjoyed a resurgence in influence and popularity when Matthew Hale took over the organization in 1995; he also claimed the title of Pontifex Maximus. Within a few years, Hale had organized dozens of new chapters across the United States. He made regular appearances in the popular media and was considered one of the more important racist leaders in the country.

By the early 2000s, however, the Creativity Movement began to collapse again. Hale was convicted of attempting to solicit the murder of a judge in 2004, and remains in prison for that crime. The Creativity Movement still exists and has active chapters in several states, but it is not one of the more significant groups in contemporary white nationalism, and it is rarely referenced in Alt-Right material.

### What Does RaHoWa Mean?

The term *RaHoWa* originated in earlier white nationalist circles, but some extreme elements of the Alt-Right have also embraced it. RaHoWa stands for "racial holy war." Ben Klassen developed the catchphrase for the Church of the Creator. RaHoWa was also the name of a white supremacist heavy metal band that released music in the early 1990s. The term is not as prevalent as *1488*, but it is used regularly by white nationalists on social media and on message boards.

## What Does ZOG Mean?

Among white nationalists, *ZOG* stands for "Zionist Occupied Government." It is based on the conspiracy theory that Jews control the U.S. government and other powerful institutions. The term was popular among twentieth-century white nationalists, and the Alt-Right still uses it in essays and forums, as well as on social media.

## What Is the Atomwaffen Division?

The Atomwaffen Division (AWD) is a new group, formed in 2015. Despite forming only recently, its style and rhetoric are more like that of the hate groups of White Nationalism 1.0 than the Alt-Right, which is why the group is included in this chapter. AWD expresses contempt for the Alt-Right's "keyboard warriors" and demands that its members step away from their computers and prepare for real-world violence. Its propaganda materials present extreme imagery without a hint of irony. AWD was an offshoot of a now-defunct website called *Iron March*.

AWD expresses admiration for several of the major figures of white nationalism, such as George Lincoln Rockwell and William Pierce. The group is also fascinated with Charles Manson, who led an infamous murderous cult in the 1960s. AWD's most important text is a collection of newsletters written by a neo-Nazi named James Mason in the 1980s. These newsletters were subsequently compiled into a book called *SIEGE*, in which Mason expressed his admiration for Manson, as well as Anton LaVey, the founder of the Church of Satan.

AWD mostly avoids the kinds of public demonstrations associated with other white nationalist groups and, more recently, the Alt-Right. It has conducted small flier campaigns on multiple college campuses. Although Alt-Right groups such as Identity Evropa also have flier campaigns, AWD fliers are more threatening, including slogans such as "Join your local Nazis" and "Prepare for race war." The fliers strongly imply that the group is prepared to engage in violent acts. AWD also emphasizes that its members are engaging in regular military training, and the group will accept only members willing to meet in the real world.

AWD members have already been tied to multiple murders. At the time of this writing, the organization has been connected to five killings, although two of these deaths were allegedly the result of one AWD member killing his own roommates, who were also members of the group. Because of its violent messages, talk of race war, and insistence that its members leave the Internet and act in the real world, AWD is potentially one of the most dangerous white nationalist groups in the United States.

### Who Is David Duke?

David Duke is among the most well known white nationalists in the United States. He is notable because he is one of the few people in the white nationalist movement to hold a significant elected office. He began working in racial politics at a young age, joining the KKK at seventeen. He later served as a Grand Wizard in the organization. While a student at Louisiana State University, he founded a group called the White Youth Alliance. He was also a member of the National Socialist Liberation Front, which began as the youth wing of the National Socialist White People's Party—known as the American Nazi Party until 1967. In 1980, he formed a new organization called the National Association for the Advancement of White People and cut ties with the KKK.

Over the last four decades, Duke has repeatedly entered the political arena. During the 1970s, he ran as a Democrat, seeking a seat in the Louisiana Senate in 1975 and 1979. He briefly sought the Democratic Party's presidential nomination in 1980, and again in 1988. After gaining a minuscule amount of support from Democratic supporters, he left the Democratic Party and ran for president on the Populist Party ticket in 1988. Although Duke never disavowed his association with hate groups, he did downplay his racism during his later electoral bids, noting that he became less radical as he grew older. He continued to focus on racial issues, but he usually emphasized subjects that mainstream Southern conservatives wanted to talk about, such as affirmative action and welfare policy.

Duke changed parties again in 1989 and ran in a special election for a seat in the Louisiana House of Representatives as a Republican. That campaign ended with Duke's sole general-election victory. He pursued a seat in the U.S. Senate in 1990 (earning a little less than 44 percent of the vote) and ran for governor of Louisiana in 1991 (earning 39 percent of the vote). Duke sought the presidency in 1992, entering the Republican primaries, though he again performed poorly. Duke ran for the U.S. Senate once more in 1996, this time winning less than 12 percent of the vote, and for the U.S. House in 1999, winning about 19 percent of the vote.

David Duke's political career is an important moment in the history of the Republican Party. His main political efforts occurred at a time when the GOP was trying to distance itself from open racists. Had he entered the U.S. Senate or the Louisiana governor's mansion, he would have been a significant albatross for the GOP. Despite winning support from Republican voters in primary elections in Louisiana, leading Republicans such as President George H.W. Bush denounced him, as did Buckley of *National Review*.

David Duke retreated from the political arena in the early 2000s. He earned a PhD in history from a private university in Ukraine in 2005. He continued writing and broadcasting racist material during this period, but his influence in the white nationalist movement waned. Early Alt-Right material rarely mentioned him.

Duke again entered the public spotlight in the context of the 2016 presidential election. He enthusiastically endorsed Donald Trump, who was subsequently criticized for not immediately disavowing Duke's support. Hoping to capitalize on Trump's movement, Duke again ran for U.S. Senate in Louisiana in 2016, but he won only about 3 percent of the vote.

Duke has since become a more significant figure within the Alt-Right. He attended the "Unite the Right" rally in Charlottesville, and shortly thereafter appeared in a video with Mike Enoch of *The Daily Shoah*. He has also appeared on another podcast hosted at *The Right Stuff* (see the section "What Is *The Right Stuff?*" in chapter 4).

### What Is the Neo-Confederate Movement?

Neo-Confederates, also known as *Southern nationalists,* want to see the results of the Civil War reversed. Although they do not all agree on the details, they would like to see the eleven states that formed the Confederate States of America between 1861 and 1865 once again have their independence.

Neo-Confederates have made many arguments. Some are not based on race. For example, some apologists for the Confederacy argue that the real issue of the Civil War was states' rights. Others engage in revisionist history, arguing that race and slavery were not the fundamental issues of that conflict.

Many contemporary Southern nationalists are also white nationalists. That is, they hope that a new and independent Southern nation would also be a white nation. The explicitly racial Southern nationalist groups may be considered part of the Alt-Right, broadly defined, although Southern nationalists existed long before the term *Alt-Right* was created. These groups include The League of the South and Identity

Dixie. These groups do not downplay the racial aspects of the Southern secession and the Civil War.

Compared to the rest of the Alt-Right, Southern nationalists tend to more heavily emphasize their Christian heritage. A blogger who uses the name "Hunter Wallace" is one of the leading voices of this movement, and Michael Hill, president of The League of the South, is another significant figure. The connection between Southern nationalism and the Alt-Right became more explicit in 2017, when the removal of statues honoring Confederate leaders was the stated catalyst for the "Unite the Right" rally.

Not all Southern heritage groups call for secession, or even have a political agenda. Some Southern heritage groups, such as the Sons of Confederate Veterans, are primarily focused on celebrating Southern history and maintaining Southern symbols in public spaces. Although these groups are controversial, their political agenda differs from that of the Alt-Right and other white nationalist movements.

### What Is Highbrow White Nationalism?

Not all white nationalists fit the stereotypes associated with the Klan or skinheads. Many far-right voices attempt to make a more scholarly case for their views. What I call *highbrow white nationalism* avoids the pageantry and violent threats typically associated with racist organizations, instead preferring journals that use academic jargon. This category of white nationalists works to revive many of the ideas about race and eugenics that were common during the Progressive era (see the section "What Was the Progressive Movement of the Late Nineteenth and Early Twentieth Centuries?" in chapter 4), and it is eager to highlight any new scientific research indicating that race is a legitimate biological category—and its proponents do so even when the researchers themselves deny any such implications for their work.

Beyond scientific issues, however, this group takes an interest in philosophers whose work validates their worldview. They strive to popularize ideas and thinkers that are otherwise mostly ignored, especially ideas developed in Europe in the interwar period and by the European New Right (see the section "Who Is Alain de Benoist, and What Is the European New Right?" in chapter 3). As is the case with most white nationalists, highbrow white nationalists are mostly found online. However, some groups also release print publications.

Like other varieties of white nationalism and related radicalism, there is relatively little financial support for those promoting these ideas. The Pioneer Fund is the most significant source of funds for individuals backing scientific racism. This group was founded in the 1930s and was explicitly in favor of eugenics. Since that time, it has funded some of the most notorious studies of race and IQ, which are frequently endorsed and promoted by white nationalists in the United States and elsewhere.

Unlike most of the groups discussed in this chapter, highbrow white nationalism has a direct and acknowledged influence on the broader Alt-Right. Examples of highbrow white nationalism include Jared Taylor's website, *American Renaissance*; the North American New Right (NANR) (see the section "What Is the North American New Right?" in chapter 3) and its website, *Counter Currents*; *The Occidental Quarterly*; and *The Occidental Observer*.

### Who Is Jared Taylor, and What Is American Renaissance?

Although it was created in the early 1990s, at a time when White Nationalism 1.0 was at a peak, we may now consider Jared Taylor's website *American Renaissance* part of the Alt-Right. Taylor founded an organization called the New Century Foundation in 1990, which is best known for producing *American Renaissance*, which was a print publication until 2013; it is now entirely online. Taylor's first book on race relations,

*Paved with Good Intentions,* was released by a mainstream publisher in 1992. Taylor's organization at one point enjoyed financial backing from the pro-eugenics Pioneer Fund.

Taylor promotes a different variety of white nationalism than other figures who were prominent in the movement in the 1990s. He avoids racial slurs and does not allow them to appear on his website. The articles in *American Renaissance* are well edited and often maintain an academic tone. The New Century Foundation regularly releases a publication titled "The Color of Crime," which looks at crime statistics broken down by race. Much of *American Renaissance* is focused on so-called race realism (see the section "What Is Race Realism?" in chapter 4), though it also prints articles on politics and culture. The website now also posts videos and podcasts.

Taylor hosts a regular *American Renaissance* conference, which brings together some of the most well known white nationalists and race realists. Speakers at these events are usually from the less radical wing of the movement—people such as Peter Brimelow of *VDARE* and John Derbyshire, who previously wrote for *National Review. VDARE* is an anti-immigration website named for Virginia Dare, the first English child born in North America.

Taylor is also distinct from both 1990s white nationalists and most of the contemporary Alt-Right, in that he rejects anti-Semitism and does not publish anti-Semitic material. He has stated on multiple occasions that he does not consider Jewish people a hindrance to his goals, and he condemns Holocaust deniers and neo-Nazis. This is a controversial position in the white nationalist movement, as anti-Semitism is often a fundamental element of their ideology. At the 2006 *American Renaissance* conference, for example, there was a heated and public argument between David Duke and one of Taylor's Jewish supporters. Although *American Renaissance* opposes anti-Semitism, *American Renaissance* conferences do not bar people from attending simply for being anti-Semites.

Taylor has more recently had disputes with the Alt-Right over the question of neo-Nazism. He was one of the most significant figures associated with the Alt-Right to denounce the use of Nazi salutes at the 2016 National Policy Institute (NPI) conference (see the section "What Is the National Policy Institute?" in chapter 6).

### What Is the White Nationalist Attitude Toward Popular Culture?

White nationalists and other racist groups have long despised mainstream popular culture. In this regard, they are like many mainstream conservatives, who also express misgivings about contemporary music, film, and literature. White nationalists, however, tend to fixate on different aspects of popular culture than do mainstream conservatives. White nationalists consider it a problem that many Jewish people have prominent positions in Hollywood, and they argue that Jews use those positions to push an antiwhite agenda—promoting multiculturalism, immigration, and interracial romantic relationships. Like conservatives, they often lambaste the entertainment industry for promoting sexual and other kinds of immorality, but this is secondary to racial issues.

White nationalists have approached the subject of popular culture from different angles. Some have attempted to create pro-white alternatives to popular forms of media. White Power music, popular among some skinhead subcultures in the 1980s and 1990s, was one means of spreading white nationalist messages. Bands such as Screwdriver developed a considerable following during this time. The National Alliance took a leading role in spreading this material after it acquired Resistance Records.

White Power music is less prevalent within the Alt-Right than it was during earlier waves of white nationalist organizing. Whereas album sales were once a source of considerable income for white nationalist groups, that is no longer the case. The rise of the Internet was one reason for this decline. With so much music available for free online, people who wanted to listen to racist music no longer needed to order albums from catalogs. The Alt-Right often creates controversies about popular culture in order to draw attention to itself. This is one of its more effective strategies for gaining media attention. For example, online Alt-Right personalities sought to organize a boycott of the *Star Wars* movie *Rogue One*, on the grounds that its creators were pushing an implicitly antiwhite, anti-Trump agenda. The hashtag #DumpStarWars was used thousands of times on Twitter. The boycott was unsuccessful, and *Rogue One* ultimately made over $1 billion. However, these kinds of stunts are useful to the Alt-Right, even when they fail in their purported goal. Just by trying to get a hashtag to trend, the Alt-Right was able to call attention to itself, earning considerable coverage from major media outlets. For an introduction to how white nationalists engage with popular culture, I recommend *Beyond Hate*, by Richard King and David Leonard.

### Were Earlier White Nationalists Part of a Global Movement, or Were They Primarily Focused in the United States?

From the beginning, American white nationalists aspired to create a global movement that would unite whites in a common struggle. Francis Parker Yockey organized overseas and was briefly associated with the British fascist Oswald Mosley. Revilo P. Oliver occasionally corresponded with Alain de Benoist (see the section "Who Is Alain de Benoist, and What Is the European New Right?" in chapter 3). Later white nationalist leaders, such as Pierce and Klassen, boasted that their organizations had chapters in several countries. Tom Metzger worked with White Power groups in Canada. Harold Covington spent some time in Africa with groups that wanted to maintain white supremacy in Rhodesia and South Africa. The NSM claims chapters in multiple countries as well.

Although it is true that many American white nationalists had international connections, we should not overstate the scale of this movement. In all the places where they existed, white nationalist organizations were small and marginalized. Although different groups may operate under the same banner, there seems to be little in the way of coordination, nor are they able to provide much in the way of mutual assistance to each other.

### What Were the Divides Within Twentieth-Century White Nationalism?

We can speak of early white nationalism as a movement, but it was never unified. Different leaders had their own groups of followers, and these leaders often had acrimonious relationships with each other. They disagreed on questions about American patriotism, religion, recruitment, and tactics.

We may accurately describe Francis Parker Yockey as the father of contemporary white nationalism, but the movement did not universally adopt his views. George Lincoln Rockwell despised Yockey's anti-Americanism, as well as his soft stance on communism. David Duke was similarly critical of Yockey's work. These white nationalists were ordinary conservatives on most issues unrelated to race.

Revilo P. Oliver and Ben Klassen hated supernatural religion, and thus argued against anyone who sought to add a spiritual element to white nationalism. This put them at odds with white nationalist Christians, including those who adopted the racist Christian Identity beliefs. It was also a problem for white nationalist pagans, who worshiped pre-Christian European gods.

These groups were also divided on whom they should recruit. In the 1980s and 1990s, some white nationalist leaders—such as Klassen and Metzger—wanted to incorporate skinheads into their movement. Pierce opposed this idea, insisting that the movement would continue to fail as long as it attracted what he called "defective" people.[7] He later said that he was glad the Creativity Movement existed, as it attracted the worst people to it and kept them from joining the National Alliance. Pierce did not consistently insist that he only wanted to attract the best and brightest, however. His music label, Resistance Records, clearly targeted a downscale audience.

Many of these feuds were simply personal disputes between would-be leaders and had little ideological content. It was common for different voices in the movement to accuse each other of being secret FBI informants or some form of controlled opposition. Notable figures also regularly accused each other of being secret Jews. Most of the major groups discussed in this chapter were built around the charisma of a single personality. As such, they rarely long survived the death or imprisonment of their leaders.

### Is the Alt-Right Just an Outgrowth of White Nationalism 1.0?

In the sense that it is driven by the same ideological goals, we can think of the Alt-Right as simply the latest manifestation of the white nationalist movement. However, we should not overstate the degree to which there is continuity between the Alt-Right and its ideological antecedents. Very few people in the Alt-Right refer to older white nationalist leaders and groups as their inspiration. In fact, many people in the Alt-Right have never even heard of them.

The highbrow white nationalists are one of the few points of direct continuity between the Alt-Right and older manifestations of these ideas. Jared Taylor was a leading voice in white nationalism in the 1990s and remains so today. The website *Counter Currents* (see the section "Who Is Alain de Benoist, and What Is the European New Right?") publishes articles by and about earlier white nationalists, like Pierce,

Oliver, and Yockey, alongside current Alt-Right material. Because much of its audience includes contemporary Alt-Right supporters, *Counter Currents* is one of the more important bridges between today's white nationalists and their twentieth-century predecessors.

### What Does the Alt-Right Think of White Nationalism 1.0?

Within the Alt-Right, there are varying opinions about the movement's predecessors. In its early days, when it was still almost entirely online, the Alt-Right sought to create distance between itself and groups like the American Nazi Party and its successors. It wanted to present itself as something genuinely new, and some of its leading figures criticized online neo-Nazis, who continued to use symbols and rhetoric associated with older generations of white nationalists. Richard Spencer, for example, banned Matthew Heimbach of the TWP from the 2014 NPI conference. Many figures in the Alt-Right routinely criticized Andrew Anglin of *The Daily Stormer* for his open radicalism and embrace of Nazi images.

By the end of 2016, however, the more radical elements of the Alt-Right seemed to have gained the upper hand, and it became less conspicuously different from earlier white nationalist movements. A problem for radical movements is that they tend to become defined by their most outrageous and extreme elements. The most radical voices are typically the ones that make the news, and thus they get to define how the overall public perceives the movement. The radicals can also be hostile to more moderate voices within their ranks, attacking them for their cowardice or lack of ideological purity. In the case of the Alt-Right, those who call for a more measured approach to propaganda and outreach are accused of "cucking" (see the section "What Does the Alt-Right Mean by *Cuckservative*?" in chapter 7) and "punching right."

## Is the Alt-Right Really That Distinct from White Nationalism 1.0?

The Alt-Right likes to view itself as a new phenomenon, representing a break from its ideological ancestors. There is some truth to this. The movement has developed some new tactics, and its overall tone differs from earlier white nationalism, especially if we compare it to white nationalism from the 1980s or 1990s.

Many important white nationalist leaders in the twentieth century believed that the movement required a religious foundation, even when they themselves had no supernatural beliefs. Most rejected mainstream Christianity and either supported the heretical Christian Identity movement or some alternative that they hoped would replace Christianity, such as Cosmotheism, Creativity, or pre-Christian paganism. Most prominent Alt-Right figures are also non-Christians, and they are often highly critical of Christianity, though there are Alt-Right Christians. However, unlike earlier white nationalists, the Alt-Right is mostly indifferent to religious questions. The movement's primary organizers and propagandists mostly avoid religious debates, viewing them as unnecessarily divisive.

Much of the Alt-Right presents its racism in an ironic manner, raising questions about its sincerity. It is not always clear if an Alt-Right supporter spreading a racist or anti-Semitic message is being genuine or just saying outrageous things for shock value. This was not the case with Klassen and Pierce; no reasonable person could question whether they meant every word they said. Within the Alt-Right, however, there are people who troll others online, simply for the nihilistic pleasure of sowing discord.

However, we should not overstate the degree to which this is a genuinely new strategy. Racist groups have engaged in similar behavior in the past. There was a farcical aspect to the Reconstruction-era KKK. Most people assume that Klan costumes were intended to both intimidate others and hide the identities of individual members. However, there was another reason for the Klan's performative elements. According to historian Elaine Frantz Parsons, the absurd nature of the Klan's costumes and hierarchy served another purpose: "Klansmen had everything to gain by encouraging northerners to read their attacks as theatrical, rather than political or military."[8] Although the KKK's white robes are well remembered, Klansmen sometimes dressed in women's clothes while persecuting former slaves.

Also like the Alt-Right, the original Klan was only loosely organized. Although figures like Nathan Bedford Forrest are remembered as the KKK's leaders, small groups calling themselves Klansmen but not directly connected to any centralized leadership structure popped up all over the South. Attempts to unite these disparate elements into a common organization and control the activities of people calling themselves part of the KKK were unsuccessful.

The use of outrageous humor and theatricality was also occasionally seen within twentieth-century white nationalist groups. George Lincoln Rockwell, the son of a vaudeville comedian, promoted a variety of racial hatred so extreme that people questioned whether he was serious. Rockwell drove a Volkswagen van with the words "Hate Bus" written conspicuously on the outside, and he created a small record label called "Hatenanny Records." Rockwell's ostentatious extremism, grandiose statements, and use of absurd imagery and slogans brought his tiny movement more attention that it would have otherwise earned. It is telling that Andrew Anglin considers Rockwell a model.

Despite these obvious similarities, it would be a mistake to say that the contemporary Alt-Right is a mere continuation of the older white nationalist movement in the United States. Although many of the most prominent Alt-Right figures are aware of white nationalism's history, this is not true of many of the movement's supporters. As a mostly young movement, the modal Alt-Right supporter has no memory of David Duke's serious political campaigns, nor does he remember the days when Aryan Nations, the National Alliance, or the CoTC were viewed as serious threats.

For most of its history, the Alt-Right differed from earlier white nationalist movements in that it mostly avoided real-world violence. At the time of this writing, the driver in the deadly car crash that took place at the "Unite the Right" rally is still awaiting trial. However, even if it is eventually determined that this was a deliberate and premeditated act of terrorism, it would be an anomaly. Most acts of violence involving the Alt-Right involve minor scuffles with antiracist protesters at public events. There is not, at this point, an Alt-Right equivalent of The Order. There are still organized violent hate groups, but they do not usually describe themselves as Alt-Right. To date, the Alt-Right has not organized any terror cells that we are aware of, nor have any of its members planned or carried out any high-profile assassinations.

However, the fact that the Alt-Right does not systematically engage in organized violence does not mean that the movement bears no responsibility for bias crimes when they occur. Aside from the death and injuries that occurred at the "Unite the Right" rally, we can find other examples of people who engaged in deadly racial violence after consuming Alt-Right online material. For instance, Dylann Roof, the Charleston church shooter, appears to have commented on articles at *The Daily Stormer*.[9]

Furthermore, we should not discount the possibility that the Alt-Right will turn more openly violent at some point. When prominent voices in the Alt-Right denounce violence, they usually do so for pragmatic reasons, rather than on principle. They avoid violence because it is, at this time, viewed as counterproductive. It would alienate its potential supporters and harm the movement's reputation, as was the case for the militia movement, which never recovered from the public outrage that followed the Oklahoma City bombing. Legal actions following violent acts have dealt white nationalist groups devastating blows in the past (see the section "Are Lawsuits an Effective Tool Against the Extreme Right?" in chapter 10), and the movement's current leaders want to avoid such problems in the future. However, we can question whether Alt-Right leaders—to the extent that they even exist—will be able to control the movement's most dangerous and unstable elements.

# 3

# RACIST MOVEMENTS ABROAD AND THE ALT-RIGHT

## How Do Far-Right Movements in Europe Differ from Those in the United States?

We can find the same ideas that motivate the Alt-Right on the other side of the Atlantic. However, the far right tends to manifest in different forms in Europe. One key difference is that far-right movements in Europe are more likely to form viable political parties. The electoral system in the United States, which has single-member, plurality-rule districts, is biased in favor of a two-party system. Although third parties exist in the United States—including openly racist parties—they have little chance of ever winning major elections or directly influencing policy. The electoral systems in most European countries are more amenable to a multiparty system, and thus far-right parties can enter national legislatures even if they win only a small percentage of the vote.

American white nationalists do not have access to viable third parties. They have no choice but to work within the existing two-party system, or else they stay out of partisan politics entirely. The 2016 presidential election was an anomaly, in that the far right was genuinely excited about a major-party presidential candidate, Donald Trump (see the section "Why Was the Alt-Right So Energized by Donald Trump?" in chapter 8). White nationalists showed no enthusiasm for Bob

Dole, George W. Bush, John McCain, or Mitt Romney. Some white nationalists, such as Louis Andrews, who helped found the National Policy Institute (NPI), even supported Barack Obama in 2008, under the theory that an African American president would speed up racial polarization.[1]

In Europe, far-right political parties such as the National Front in France, the Freedom Party of Austria, and the Sweden Democrats have made significant electoral gains. In Poland and Hungary, such parties are now dominant. Xenophobic, right-wing populist parties now appear to be a permanent fixture of European electoral politics, and right-wing energies in those countries are now being channeled into these parties. Unless the Alt-Right manages to capture the GOP, which I consider unlikely despite Donald Trump's victory (see the section "Can the Alt-Right Copy the Conservative Model and Take Over the Republican Party?" in chapter 7), this does not appear to be a viable model for it. This section, therefore, will not discuss these far-right European political parties in any detail. I will instead focus on those groups and individuals that have had a more direct effect on the Alt-Right's views and strategies.

Although the American extreme right does not control any significant political parties, it has one possible advantage over its European counterparts: the First Amendment. Hate speech laws are common throughout Europe, and public expressions of bigotry can result in severe punishment. Those who wish to spread intolerance in Europe, therefore, must choose their words very carefully or risk criminal charges. This is not the case in the United States, where right-wing radicals are free to march down the street carrying swastika flags. In the United States, so long as these groups are not explicitly calling for specific acts of violence, they are free to spread their message in public forums.

But one can question whether greater free speech protection actually helps the American far right. Although costumed American neo-Nazis and Klansmen can acquire permits and hold public rallies and parades, there is scant evidence that these displays draw large numbers of new recruits. Indeed, such events can alienate many Americans, even those who exhibit high levels of racial resentment and anxiety. For this reason, it is not surprising that some Alt-Right groups—notably Identity Evropa (see the section "What Is Identity Evropa?" in chapter 6)—are transitioning toward the European model of far-right activism, abandoning the kinds of events associated with groups like the National Socialist Movement and such predecessors as the American Nazi Party.

### What Is Fascism?

Political pundits and other public figures on all sides of the political spectrum frequently use the term *fascist* to describe their opponents. In fact, the word is so commonly used that it seems to have lost any real meaning. Some progressives accused George W. Bush of fascism,[2] and the conservative columnist Jonah Goldberg accuses liberals of having latent fascistic leanings.[3]

If we insist on absolute precision when using the term *fascist*, we should probably limit its application exclusively to members of the National Fascist Party in Benito Mussolini's Italy. That would also be unsatisfactory, as the tendencies within Mussolini's regime were certainly present elsewhere, and we can broadly define many movements as fascist, or at least fascistic. My own preferred definition of *fascism* comes from Roger Griffin, one of the world's leading experts on fascism:

> Fascism is a revolutionary species of political modernism originating in the early 20th century whose mission is to combat the allegedly degenerate forces of contemporary history (decadence) by bringing about an alternative modernity and temporality (a "new order"

and a "new era") based on the rebirth, or palingenisis, of the nation. Fascists coneive the nation as an organism shaped by historic, cultural, and in some cases, ethnic and hereditary forces, a mythic construct incompatible with liberal, conservative, and communist theories of society. The health of the organism they see undermined as much by the principles of institutional pluralism, individualism, and globalized consumerism promoted by liberalism as by the global regime of social justice and human equality identified by socialism in theory as the ultimate goal of history, or by the conservative defense of "tradition."[4]

Donald Trump's opponents have described him as a fascist since he launched his presidential run. There were elements of Trump's campaign that seem to match this definition. The slogan "Make America Great Again" does sound like a call to national rebirth. Trump is also certainly a nationalist, which puts him at odds with both contemporary conservatism and liberalism. However, Trump does not fit this definition in other ways. Trump does not reject individualism, for example. Griffin himself rejects the argument that Trump is a fascist, noting recently, "As long as Trump does not advocate the abolition of America's democratic institutions, and their replacement by some sort of post-liberal new order, he's not technically a fascist."[5]

Not all social observers insist on such a limited definition of the word, however. The journalist Shane Burley, author of *Fascism Today*, prefers a broader definition, arguing that fascism is defined by "the belief in human inequality, the defense of some type of immobile hierarchy, and the belief in essentialized identity, identities that are fixed and define who you are. Violence, mass politics, mythology, and romanticism are all a part of this as well, and are manifested in a range of ways."[6] This definition allows a movement to be described as fascist even if it has no direct connection with mid-twentieth-century European regimes.

Whether one prefers a broad or narrow definition of fascism, however, we can reasonably describe the Alt-Right as fascistic. Although it often does so in an ironic manner, much of the Alt-Right embraces fascist and even Nazi imagery. It uses the terms *fash* or *fashy* to describe itself and the things that it likes. It seeks a rebirth of white racial consciousness. It is openly antidemocracy, although the movement does pragmatically use the democratic process when it suits its interests.

### Who Is Alain de Benoist, and What Is the European New Right?

The European New Right (ENR) was an attempt to formulate a new right-wing vision of society in the postwar era. World War II destroyed fascism's credibility, and in many countries, it became illegal to promote a return to fascism or something analogous. Nonetheless, several activists and intellectuals rejected both American liberalism and Soviet Communism, and wanted to develop a new right-wing alternative.

The ENR began in France in the late 1960s. Its birth coincided with a period in which the radical left in that country was at the peak of its strength, to the point where a left-wing revolution seemed possible. In 1968, a young, right-wing journalist named Alain de Benoist and his colleagues founded the Research and Study Group for European Civilization—better known by its French acronym, GRECE. The group sought to revive what it considered the best elements of fascism, while rejecting genocide and other forms of blatant racial and religious violence.

Although the ENR did not fully endorse the right-wing regimes that ruled much of Europe prior to 1945, it was inspired by some of the same intellectual sources. They frequently cited writers such as Carl Schmitt, Arthur Moeller van den Bruck, and other intellectuals associated with the so-called Conservative Revolutionary movement in interwar

Germany. In its early years, the ENR was transparently racist. Francis Parker Yockey's ideas influenced de Benoist and his colleagues. The ENR was different from its counterparts on the American far right, however. Over time, it began to move away from transparent racism and began to borrow language from the political left.

Like the left, the ENR expressed a strong interest in environmental conservation. The movement was overtly anticapitalist and anti-American. It hated the degree to which American culture was dominating the globe and sought to make common cause with populist, anti-American uprisings in the developing world. For example, de Benoist supported the 1979 Iranian Revolution against the pro-American shah, Mohammad Reza Pahlavi. Although the ENR's arguments against Western colonialism and cultural imperialism were superficially like those found on the left, they were based on a very different foundation.

After moving away from racialist arguments, de Benoist and others from his circle began to focus heavily on culture. Specifically, they insisted on what they called the "right to difference." That is, different cultures should have the right to develop independently and organically, without outside interference. This also applied to Europe, which they considered threatened by Americanization and the growth of non-European immigrant populations. Trends toward globalization, in their view, threatened to destroy the world's diverse and unique cultures, as all parts of the globe have increasingly become part of the same homogeneous consumer culture. The right to difference thus included a right to exclude or expel groups that threatened cultural cohesiveness.

For its exclusionary nature, the ENR was attacked by the left and political center for promoting little more than a rebranded fascism. These critiques, however, did not keep de Benoist and others from becoming important parts of the European intellectual landscape in the late twentieth century. Their ideas and work appeared in many important publications.

Anti-Christianity was another crucial element of the ENR. In this regard, the movement was similar to many American white nationalist groups, such as the National Alliance and Church of the Creator (CoTC). Although the ENR opposed Christianity for many of the same reasons as these far-right American groups, it also had some additional complaints. In keeping with his left-wing argumentation style, de Benoist lambasted Christianity for its intolerance. As is the case with other monotheistic religions, Christianity proclaims that it possesses universal truth. It claims both that it is open to everyone, and that every other religion is false. Thus, de Benoist argued that Christianity is, by its very nature, totalitarian, and even those totalitarian regimes that were formally atheist nonetheless had Christian cultural roots.

The ENR contrasted Christianity with pre-Christian European paganism, in which people tolerated a multiplicity of gods according to local customs. According to this view, religious tolerance and diversity were the norm throughout Europe until the Roman Empire converted to Christianity and began to stamp out other religious identities. Although the ENR did not call on its adherents to actually worship ancient gods, it argued that returning Europeans to a pre-Christian mindset was an important part of their cultural struggle.

The ENR, for the most part, remained aloof from partisan politics. Engaging with elections necessarily involves making compromises to maximize a party's total number of votes. The ENR had a more ambitious agenda. The Italian Marxist Antonio Gramsci influenced de Benoist and others in his circle. According to Gramsci, true and lasting political change is possible only if it is preceded by a cultural change. This was one reason that socialist revolutionaries were regularly unsuccessful in the early twentieth century; the culture maintained bourgeois norms, which made a top-down revolution unsustainable.

The ENR absorbed this lesson, determining that a real right-wing revolution first required fundamentally changing the culture. Its ideas needed to become hegemonic, which meant that, for the time being, the ENR needed to focus its energy on cultural products and converting intellectuals. It did not want to be bogged down by efforts to build political coalitions around existing cultural conditions. Engaging in premature partisan politics would require them to dilute their ideological message—especially as it pertains to issues like Christianity. Alain de Benoist's primary goal was influencing what he called metapolitics—the overall worldview that undergirds a political culture.

By the 1990s, the ENR's influence seemed to be waning. It continued to face heated criticism from the left, which maintained its stance that the ENR was just trying to normalize fascistic and other intolerant ideas. It also faced challenges from the right, from voices that viewed de Benoist's emphasis on highbrow metapolitics as ineffectual, doing little to reverse the cultural and demographic changes that the far right opposed.

Alain de Benoist maintains that he has little direct connection with the Alt-Right and similar movements.[7] However, he has shown no apparent hesitation to collaborate with white nationalists. He has spoken at NPI conferences, for example, and Richard Spencer cites him as an important inspiration. Arktos Media, which is now part of the Alt-Right Corporation (see the section "What Is the Alt-Right Corporation?" in chapter 6), is responsible for translating many of de Benoist's books into English.

### Who Is Guillaume Faye?

Although many voices within the Alt-Right express admiration for de Benoist, Guillaume Faye, who has been critical of de Benoist for decades, has arguably had a greater influence on the Alt-Right than any other figure associated with the ENR. Faye previously collaborated with de Benoist, but the relationship soured in the 1980s. Faye concluded that de Benoist's metapolitical strategy was not working, and the right needed to be more aggressive, transparent, and willing to act in the real world.

Faye rejected the idea that his movement was driven by a universalist desire to preserve all distinct people. Instead, he was open about caring exclusively about white Europeans. He further argued that pretending to care about the rest of the globe was counterproductive; doing so waters down their core message, and their opponents will call them fascists anyway. According to Faye, Europeans do not have time to slowly change the culture with abstract arguments. He views immigration into Europe—particularly from majority-Muslim countries—as an immediate and existential threat. For this reason, he wants immigration to stop and reverse itself. Whereas de Benoist now says that Muslims in Europe should be allowed to maintain their own "right to difference," Faye wants to remove them from the continent entirely.

Faye believes that the United States has deliberately sought to weaken Europe, and that it promotes Muslim immigration as a way to do so, but he is less focused on anti-Americanism than de Benoist. Although he shares de Benoist's distaste for the growing American cultural dominance in Europe, he finds this less threatening to Europe's long-term survival than non-white immigration. Although the ENR overall is disturbed by the increasing presence of both McDonald's restaurants and Muslim minarets in Europe, Faye is far more worried about the latter. Although Faye is not a Christian, and is often critical of Christianity, he disagrees with de Benoist's argument that Christianity is ultimately to blame for current ideological trends in Europe. Nor does he consider anti-Christianity a core element of his political program. He is also willing to state that his concern is racial rather than cultural.

Faye's writing is decidedly apocalyptic, and he argues that the modern world is unsustainable. In his book, *Convergence of Catastrophes*, he argued that environmental degradation, over-population, the depletion of fossil fuels, terrorism, and global debt will bring down modern societies. Although this collapse will be painful, and a huge percentage of the global population will die in the process, it will ultimately destroy liberalism as an ideology.

For his open racism and radicalism, authorities have prosecuted Faye for hate speech. His book, *The Colonization of Europe*, was the catalyst for this prosecution. There, Faye openly called for the "reconquest" of Europe and explained the necessity of a civil war—which he hoped would begin shortly.

Faye has influenced the extreme right in both Europe and the United States. He has spoken at a NPI conference and an *American Renaissance* conference. His work is promoted by the American white nationalist group Identity Evropa. The white nationalist website *Counter Currents* has translated many of Faye's shorter essays, and Arktos has translated and published several of his books.

Although Faye is well respected by many leading white nationalists in the United States, they tend to break with him on the question of Israel and anti-Semitism. Faye is a strong supporter of Israel and argues against those white nationalists who blame Jewish people for trends they view as deleterious.

### What Is Traditionalism?

The Traditionalist School is one of the more curious influences on both the ENR and the Alt-Right. Many thinkers are associated with this intellectual movement, but René Guénon and Julius Evola have had the most significant influence on the right. The connection between Traditionalism and the modern far right may not be immediately clear. The Traditionalist School contends that the modern world is totally degenerate, representing the low point of a historical cycle—what Hindus call the *Kali Yuga*, a period when people are cut off from real spirituality.

Traditionalism advances the idea, known as *perennialism*, that all true religions spring from the same transcendent source.

Unlike most modern far-right movements, Traditionalism is not Islamophobic. Guénon eventually converted to Sufi Islam and moved to Egypt.

Evola's impact on the far right is more apparent than Guénon's. Born into an aristocratic Sicilian family in 1898, he became one of the most radically right-wing intellectuals of the twentieth century. Unlike Guénon, who mostly avoided politics, Evola was an influential thinker in fascist Italy and Nazi Germany. He was a radical antiegalitarian and hostile to Christianity, preferring religious traditions he considered more masculine and hierarchical. Like the ENR, as well as some contemporary white nationalists, Evola hated the United States and its bourgeois values. He did not view the United States and the Soviet Union as ideological opposites. Instead, they represented two slightly different variations of the same modern mindset.

Evola often criticized fascism, but his complaint was always that it was insufficiently radical. In his view, Mussolini's Italy was too egalitarian and too contaminated by modernity. He admired the German Schutzstaffel (SS), but he took issue with other elements of Hitler's Germany. He also wrote fondly about the Romanian Iron Guard. After World War II, when the Allied victory dashed his hopes that a new, more traditionalist order was possible, Evola withdrew from political activity but continued to write about politics, culture, and religion.

*Revolt Against the Modern World, Men Among the Ruins*, and *Ride the Tiger* were Evola's most significant political books. Evola died in 1974, though his works continue to inspire right-wing movements.

Alt-Right literature often references Traditionalist ideas. Evola has become a meme in the Alt-Right—though it is questionable that many contemporary Alt-Right supporters are well versed in his strange religious theories, which were central to his worldview. Richard Spencer has written favorably about Evola, and many of his essays have been translated and posted on the *Counter Currents* website. Steve Bannon (see the section

"Who Is Steve Bannon?" in chapter 9) has also expressed admiration for Evola and Guénon.

For an introduction to Traditionalism, I recommend Mark Sedgwick's book, *Against the Modern World*.

### What Is the North American New Right?

The North American New Right (NANR) is a movement primarily associated with Greg Johnson, an American white nationalist—but it may be an overstatement to call it a movement. It is mostly associated with the website that Johnson edits called *Counter Currents*, which publishes many original pieces, as well as translations from European far-right authors. Johnson also oversees the publication of books and a print journal, also called *North American New Right*—though to date, only two editions of the print journal have been released. Although it is an American initiative, led by Americans, it is appropriate to include it in this chapter because of its European intellectual roots.

Compared to the ENR, the NANR is more explicit in its racism and anti-Semitism. Johnson, for example, is an explicit white nationalist, and his site has republished articles from some of the most radical figures from the racist right, such as Ben Klassen, William Pierce, and George Lincoln Rockwell. This may be due to the different legal climates in Europe and the United States—American venues have more free speech protection. Much of the site's material focuses on the infamous, so-called Jewish Question. The site itself, however, states that the NANR rejects totalitarianism and genocide.

The NANR does not just produce essays and podcasts on politics and philosophy; much of its output focuses on popular culture, critiqued from a white nationalist perspective. Regular discussion of well-known films and television programs is common within the Alt-Right. This makes strategic sense, as these topics interest most Americans, and by engaging with these subjects, they can reach out to a larger audience.

Like the ENR, the NANR describes its efforts as metapolitical. That is, it does not engage in traditional political activism, nor does it troll on social media. Like the ENR, the NANR is mostly uninterested in partisan electoral politics. The group's goal is to spread its ideas among a more intellectual audience, with the hope that they eventually become normal and even dominant.

### What Is the Identitarian Movement?

The Identitarian movement is an extension of the ENR. The group Génération Identitaire, the youth wing of the Bloc Identitaire, was founded in France in 2012, and it now has chapters throughout Europe. Like the Alt-Right, the Identitarian movement tries to rhetorically and stylistically distance itself from older far-right movements, though its ultimate goals are similar. Like other European far-right groups, they are particularly preoccupied with the question of Muslim immigration.

The Identitarian movement is known for its use of the *flash mob*, in which a small number of activists rapidly occupy a space, make an argument, and disperse before authorities and counterprotesters can respond. They first earned international attention when they briefly occupied a mosque in the French city of Poitiers. They chose this location because it was the site of Charles Martel's victory over an invading Muslim army in the year 732. Identitarians have made headlines more recently with their plans to disrupt nongovernmental organization (NGO) ships carrying refugees into Europe. They have raised a considerable amount of money for this project.

The term *Identitarian* has become popular in the American far right—Richard Spencer, for example, uses the term to describe himself. As with the Alt-Right, an advantage to this term is that it is does not seem inherently racist. There are also increasing connections between the American Alt-Right and European Identitarian movements. The right-wing Canadian journalist Lauren Southern, for example, played a role in the Identitarian efforts to disrupt migrant ships. The American group Identity Evropa explicitly models itself on the European Identitarian movement.

A common refrain within the Identitarian movement is that they have been victimized by the " '68ers." This refers to the left-wing protesters who disrupted France in 1968. In their most popular online video, Génération Identitaire attacked the generation that came of age in the 1960s for its selfishness, rejection of tradition, and support for multiculturalism. The idea that today's youthful far right is responding to the older generation's egalitarianism and materialism is also common in the American Alt-Right.

### Is There Cooperation Between the Alt-Right in America and the Far Right in Europe?

There are connections between the American Alt-Right and far-right groups in Europe. This is not unique to the Alt-Right. Leading white nationalists have always tried to expand their network beyond the borders of the United States (see the section "Were Earlier White Nationalists Part of a Global Movement, or Were They Primarily Focused in the United States?" in chapter 2). The Alt-Right seems to be more successful than its predecessors in this regard, however. Some of this difference is the result of technological advances. Compared to fifty or even twenty years ago, international communication is far easier. The large number of Europeans who now speak and read English also facilitates the development of an international movement. Alt-Right memes and ideas are now spreading within right-wing European circles, and tactics honed by European Identitarian groups are now being mimicked by Americans.

We also now see far-right conferences that host speakers from many different countries. As mentioned previously, *American Renaissance* and the NPI have invited speakers associated with the European far right. The "Identitarian Ideas" conference, hosted in 2017 in Sweden, included several Americans. The far-right London Forum has also hosted many speakers from outside the United Kingdom, as has the Scandza Forum.

However, efforts to create international right-wing events have hit some roadblocks. The NPI, for example, attempted to host a conference in Budapest, Hungary, in 2014, but the Hungarian government banned the event. Richard Spencer attempted to host a gathering in that country anyway, and he was arrested and deported from the country as a result. This occurred even though Hungary arguably had the most right-wing government in Europe at the time. Poland similarly banned Spencer from entering its borders in 2017, an edict lasting five years, and because of the European Union's immigration laws, this ban extends to all other European countries in the Schengen Area as well. As with Hungary, a right-wing populist government governed Poland at the time. The United Kingdom imposed an indefinite ban on Spencer visiting that country in 2016.

As was the case with twentieth-century white nationalists, we should not overstate the significance of a growing international extreme right. Although different groups and individuals can easily make connections, these voices remain a minority in every country. The fact that people across national boundaries are talking to each other may not be particularly significant. It is notable, however, that these movements are paying attention to each other and are able to learn from their respective successes and failures.

### Is There a Connection Between the Alt-Right and Russia?

Russia has been accused of meddling in the 2016 U.S. presidential election on behalf of Donald Trump. There is evidence that Russia deliberately targeted social media to sway the election in Trump's favor, for example.[8] Key players in the Trump administration have been investigated for colluding with

Moscow. At the time of this writing, these investigations are ongoing. Whether or not President Trump himself had any knowledge of Russian interference, it does appear that the Russian government wanted him to win that election, and that it continues to seek to sow instability and distrust in American political life. Given these shared interests, one might reasonably theorize a connection between the Alt-Right and the authoritarian Russian government.

The ideological similarities between the Alt-Right and the Russian government are obvious. Many in the Alt-Right express admiration for Russian president Vladimir Putin and approved of Trump's mostly congenial relationship with him. Russian scholar Alexander Dugin, reportedly an influential voice in the Kremlin, was influenced by the ENR and has many devotees in the Alt-Right. *AltRight.com* has published multiple translations of Dugin essays, and the Alt-Right publisher Arktos has published translations of several of his books. Washington Summit Publishers has published another, which was translated by Richard Spencer's wife—who was born in Russia.

Given this overlap, it is not surprising that some people have speculated that Russia has played a role in the Alt-Right's growth. Russia has supported right-wing nationalist movements outside its borders in the past. The conservative radio host Glenn Beck, for example, has argued that the Alt-Right is just one part of a larger, right-wing, nationalist conspiracy directed by Moscow.[9]

It would not be surprising to discover that the Alt-Right received some form of assistance from Russia. However, at the time of this writing, there is no hard evidence that any major Alt-Right groups have received significant material assistance from the Russian government. Furthermore, even the proven connections between Russia and the Alt-Right have been inconsequential. For example, *The Daily Beast* discovered that a popular blogger and Twitter user who often repeated far-right talking points was not a real person, but rather created by a Russian "troll farm."[10]

It is possible that a meaningful relationship between Russia and the Alt-Right will be discovered in the future. The Alt-Right's apparent meager resources, however, indicate that any support that the movement receives is insubstantial.

Furthermore, we should not overstate the degree to which the Alt-Right's ideology matches Putin's. Although Russia has a right-wing government, it does not necessarily stand to benefit from a global surge of racial nationalism and separatism. Russia is a diverse country, containing a vast number of ethnic groups with different languages and religious traditions, and Chechen separatists were one of the most difficult problems that President Putin faced early in his presidency. The idea that distinct racial and ethnic groups are entitled to their own sovereignty is not aligned with the Russian government's interests.

# 4

# OTHER INFLUENCES ON THE ALT-RIGHT

## What Is Populism?

Like fascism or conservatism, populism is a concept that most people intuitively grasp but may not be able to define clearly. Unlike, say, libertarianism, populism is not a coherent ideology based on a series of logical axioms. Neither is it tied to a particular set of policies. The fact that both Donald Trump and Bernie Sanders were described as populists during their respective battles for presidential nominations demonstrates this idea. Yet populism is more than just a vague appeal to "the people." To be classified accurately as populist, a leader or movement should meet certain criteria. Political scientist Cas Mudde described populism as "an ideology that considers society to be ultimately separated into two homogeneous and antagonistic groups, 'the pure people' versus 'the corrupt elite,' and which argues that politics should be an expression of the *volonté générale* (general will) of the people."[1] Although populism may often be associated with a charismatic leader or leaders, it does not require a particular leadership style. Populism presents politics as more than a competition of various interests; it is fundamentally a Manichean view of the political world, in which the virtuous "people" seek to overthrow scheming and avaricious "elites."

Although all populists are defined by this simple dichotomy, populism can manifest itself in multiple ways. For this reason, in contrast to other political frameworks, it is a "thin ideology,"[2] if it can be described as an ideology at all.[3] Although the populist stands for "the people" and their interests, these perceived interests will depend on the greater context. In poorer regions of the globe, such as parts of Latin America, populism is predominantly a phenomenon of the political left, calling for greater social equity and a redistribution of resources. In economically developed countries, populism is typically found on the political right, where populists defend "the people" from both globalist elites and Third-World immigrants.

Unlike most center-right politicians and parties, the right-wing populist is skeptical of big business, viewing its desire for cheap, immigrant labor as a threat to the nation's cultural integrity. Beyond attacking official power-holders, the political and economic elite, the populist is also hostile to those that shape and advance the elites' values, especially the media and academia.[4] We see examples of this variety of populism throughout Western Europe, particularly in political parties such as the National Front in France and the UK Independence Party (UKIP) in the United Kingdom. We have recently seen it in the United States in the candidacy of Donald Trump, though we also witnessed earlier manifestations of it in the candidacies of George Wallace, Ross Perot, and Pat Buchanan. Michael P. Ferderici provided a helpful definition of right-wing populism, especially as it manifests itself in the United States:

> Right-wing populism is less concerned with consumer and environmental issues and more concerned with social and economic issues. School prayer, abortion, tuition tax credits, privatization, and tax cuts are common issues of right-wing populism. Right-wing populists, deviating

from the tradition of Rousseau, are apt to view "the people" not as a collection of individuals but as a collection of private associations. In other words, the popular will is expressed, according to the right-wing populist, through intermediate associations such as church, club, family, school, or business.[5]

The relationship between populism and democracy can be nebulous. It seems absurd to describe populists as antidemocrat, given that populists explicitly call for the rule of the majority. Indeed, the populist is more likely than other ideologues to favor decision-making via direct democracy—through referendums and popular initiatives. Yet populism also has a transparent illiberal quality, and thus it threatens other democratic values, such as minority rights.

### How Populist Is the Alt-Right?

The Alt-Right has some populist characteristics. It is strongly suspicious of Western elites, viewing them as enemies of the white race and accusing them of perpetrating a quiet campaign of genocide by encouraging nonwhite immigration, interracial relationships, low white birth rates, racial guilt, and the denigration of white culture. The Alt-Right's populist rhetoric is often implicitly or explicitly anti-Semitic. It usually argues that Jewish elites are the main drivers of the policies they oppose, and the liberal white Gentiles who also support these policies are either unwitting dupes or exhibit a pathological degree of altruism and ethnomasochism.

It would nonetheless be inappropriate to describe the Alt-Right as a populist movement, even if it sometimes uses populist rhetoric. Although the Alt-Right derides "elites," it does not celebrate the virtues of common people. The Alt-Right claims to stand for the interests of white people, but it is openly contemptuous of most whites, whom it derides as "normies." Although the movement is not in total agreement on this question, the Alt-Right would like to see one form of elite rule replaced with another—specifically, they want society to be ruled by people who share their ideology. The Alt-Right does not share the populist enthusiasm for democracy for its own sake.

## What Is Neoreaction?

Neoreaction (often abbreviated as NRx) is an ideological movement that is often equated with the Alt-Right, or at least viewed as an important precursor to it. This is understandable, as the two overlap on several important cultural and policy questions. The main voices associated with NRx, for example, tend to endorse theories of scientific racism, mostly agreeing that different racial groups have nonsuperficial differences. However, NRx writers do not typically make race their primary focus, nor does the overall movement exhibit significant anti-Semitism. They instead tend to write about the problems with democracy and other modern ideas. On many questions, NRx is even more antidemocratic and antiegalitarian than the Alt-Right.

Although the Alt-Right is predominantly online, NRx is exclusively so, though the figures associated with NRx typically do not engage in trolling. NRx is uninterested in persuading large numbers of people that its views are correct. Leading thinkers in NRx include the philosopher Nick Land and a computer scientist who wrote under the name Mencius Moldbug. Instead of tweets and podcasts, NRx writers typically prefer extraordinarily long essays—far longer than typical blog posts.

Like the Alt-Right, NRx first emerged during the George W. Bush administration, and it similarly rejected mainstream conservative thinking. Although NRx has a generally libertarian view on policy, it does not consider democracy a suitable mechanism for achieving libertarian ends. NRx writers usually promote some form of monarchical government or a society governed by technocratic elites. It argues that the world's dominant institutions, including education, the media, and government, spread disinformation and tell the public what to think; they call this cluster of institutions "the Cathedral."

Despite the many similarities between the Alt-Right and NRx, it would be incorrect to say that one spawned the other. During the Alt-Right's first iteration, in *Taki's Magazine* and *Alternative Right*, there was no significant discussion of NRx ideas, though many people read both Alt-Right and NRx material.

### What Is Paleoconservatism?

Paleoconservatism is a branch of the mainstream conservative movement, noted primarily for its antipathy to neoconservatives (see the section "What Is Neoconservatism?" in chapter 7). Paul Gottfried coined the term. As the name suggests, paleoconservatism represents an older variety of conservatism. As conservatism evolved during the latter decades of the twentieth century, the paleoconservatives maintained their earlier positions. Paleoconservatives were less willing to change their views on racial issues than other conservatives, though it would be incorrect to label paleoconservatism a white nationalist movement. Paleoconservatives strongly supported restrictive immigration policies at a time when many prominent conservatives were moving in the opposite direction. They differed from their mainstream counterparts most aggressively on matters of foreign policy, however. The paleoconservatives had no interest in foreign wars justified by abstractions like the idea of spreading democracy. They were often very critical of America's relationship with Israel, raising concerns that paleoconservatives were anti-Semites.

After bitter battles with other conservatives in the 1980s and 1990s, the paleoconservative wing of the movement was mostly banished from the mainstream conservative movement. President Ronald Reagan's decision to withdraw his nomination of the paleoconservative Mel Bradford as chair of the National Endowment for the Humanities, at the request of William F. Buckley, Jr., and other conservatives, was a critical moment (see the section "What Has Been Conservatism's Response to Open Racism in Its Ranks?" in chapter 7). This demonstrated that the conservative movement no longer needed or wanted paleoconservatives in their coalition. Following this break, paleoconservatives had few outlets for their ideas. A small magazine called *Chronicles* was, and remains, the primary outlet for paleoconservative thought.

Despite losing every major battle with neoconservatives in the 1980s, paleoconservatives nonetheless had one remaining champion with access to a major platform: Patrick J. Buchanan. In his presidential runs, Buchanan kept paleoconservative ideas in the national conversation. Buchanan had strong conservative credentials, having served in Richard Nixon's and Reagan's administrations. He was a strong supporter of the Cold War throughout that conflict. However, when the Soviet Union dissolved and the Cold War ended, Buchanan called for a massive drawdown of the U.S. military. He was an outspoken opponent of the Gulf War, and predicted the conflict would end in disaster.

Buchanan also broke with conservative dogma on the issue of free trade—he opposed it, instead wanting strong protectionist policies to defend American manufacturing. He was one of the loudest voices against undocumented immigration on the right, and an outspoken conservative Christian on all social issues. In his most famous speech, he declared, "There is a religious war going on in this country. It is a cultural war, as critical to the kind of nation we shall be as was the Cold War itself, for this war is for the soul of America."[6] Buchanan also criticized America's relationship with Israel, which some observers argued crossed the line into open anti-Semitism.

Buchanan launched a quixotic primary campaign against the incumbent president George H. W. Bush in 1992. The bid was never likely to succeed, but it did provide a chance to express paleoconservative ideas to a national audience. Buchanan made a second bid for the Republican nomination in 1996, and he won the important New Hampshire primary before being defeated by the more moderate and mainstream Robert Dole. In 2000, Buchanan ran for president a third time, as a third-party candidate. He won a negligible share of the votes and never again sought public office.

Beyond his political ambitions, Buchanan is best known for his books and columns. He maintains an alarmist tone in his written works, and his books have titles such as *The Death of the West, Day of Reckoning,* and *State of Emergency.* The dangers that mass immigration, foreign wars, and the decline of Christianity pose to the United States are a common theme in his works. His most controversial book, *Suicide of a Superpower,* seemed to cross the line into open racism, as it included a chapter titled "The End of White America." Buchanan also helped found a magazine called *The American Conservative* in 2002, which provided right-wing critiques of the Iraq War, which began in 2003.

Buchanan remains a respected figure within the Alt-Right, but the most important bridge between paleoconservatism and white nationalism was undoubtedly Sam Francis. Francis was once an important figure in the conservative movement. After earning his PhD, he worked as an analyst for the Heritage Foundation and as an aide to Republican senator John East. He later became a columnist for *The Washington Times.* The conservative intellectual James Burnham influenced Francis, who wrote a book of his own on Burnham's thought. Francis argued that the conservative movement was a failure, and that middle America needed to wage a populist revolt against governing elites, both left and right. Unlike most conservatives, Francis did not have a problem with "big government" per se, but he was alarmed that the bloated government served the interests of the poor and minorities, while forcing middle-class whites to pay the bill. Like the contemporary Alt-Right, and unlike Buchanan and other paleoconservatives, Francis never showed much interest in social issues such as school prayer or abortion. He also showed little interest in free-market capitalism.

Francis was eventually fired from the *Times* because of his racially inflammatory written remarks and for a speech he gave at the 1994 *American Renaissance* conference. After losing access to all major conservative venues, Francis continued to write for *Chronicles,* but he also began working with more explicitly white nationalist groups. He became an editor of the white nationalist journal, *The Occidental Quarterly.* Francis died in 2005, well before the term *Alt-Right* was coined. Yet his influence on the radical right is clear. Washington Summit Publishers, run by Richard Spencer, published Francis's final book, *Leviathan and Its Enemies,* in 2016.

### What Is Libertarianism?

After mainstream conservatism, libertarianism is the largest, most influential, and best-funded right-wing political movement in the United States, though some libertarians may object to being classified as right wing. Libertarians hold individual liberty as the highest political ideal, and they want government as small as possible—if they want any government at all. Although different proponents have different views about when laws and other forms of government intervention are necessary, libertarianism contends that individuals should be free to use their persons or property as they see fit, so long as they do not violate anyone else's rights. Libertarians typically make appeals to natural rights and view themselves as the most consistent heirs to the classical liberal tradition.

Libertarians often base their arguments on the *nonaggression principle,* which holds that no one has the right to violate the person or property of another person. This includes personal relationships, but it extends to government as well. To libertarians, many laws represent a form of unjust aggression.

Because libertarians believe people should enjoy the maximum amount of freedom, they oppose legal restrictions on how people can use their own bodies, such as drug prohibition and laws against prostitution. They are similarly opposed to most economic regulations, such as minimum wages. Libertarians also oppose most wars, preferring that military force be used only as a last resort. Most libertarians opposed the invasion of Iraq.

Libertarians argue among themselves about when governments can justly act. Some libertarians are genuine anarchists (also called *anarcho-capitalists,* or *AnCaps*). They believe that no government is necessary, and even things like collective defense can be handled by private actors. Most libertarians accept that government of some kind is necessary and endorse the creation of a military (which must be used only for defense), a police force, and a judiciary that can settle disputes. Others will accept the use of government to provide services such as fire departments, as we may not be able to rely on the free market to provide these kinds of nonexcludable public goods.

Libertarians disagree with each other on questions about national borders. On the one hand, libertarian ideals seem to preclude government action that blocks a willing employer from hiring a willing worker, regardless of immigration status. However, other libertarians argue that border protection is a vital task for the state. Some libertarians take a pragmatic rather than principled stance on immigration; they note that immigrants are more likely to support big government policies, and thus generous immigration policies will make it more difficult to create a libertarian order. On average, however, libertarians are more pro-immigration than conservatives.

Libertarians often partner with conservatives when their ideals are aligned. Conservatives and libertarians often have analogous views on economic questions, and libertarian organizations such as the Cato Institute wield considerable influence in conservative politics. Some of the most influential right-wing intellectuals since World War II identified as libertarian, including Milton Friedman.

Libertarians have the longest-lasting and most successful third party in the United States, the Libertarian Party, which has run a candidate in every presidential election since 1972. The most recent Libertarian presidential candidate was former New Mexico governor Gary Johnson. He won nearly 4.5 million votes in 2016, making him the most successful third-party candidate since Ross Perot.

### What Are the Connections Between Libertarianism and the Alt-Right?

Most high-profile libertarians have no interest in the Alt-Right and reject white nationalism and similar ideas. A connection between libertarianism and white nationalism may not seem immediately obvious. However, historically, libertarians have supported several policies that white nationalists also support. Libertarian principles, for example, preclude the use of government to force the racial integration of private businesses—racial discrimination committed by private businesses may be immoral and bad economics, but forcing business owners to act against their beliefs is a violation of the nonaggression principle.

In 2017, several writers published articles noting that many people in the Alt-Right previously identified as libertarians, and so they argued that there is at least a degree of latent bigotry within libertarianism.[7] This is probably an exaggeration. Most libertarians are sincerely opposed to racism and are not using antistatism as a mask for racism or other forms of prejudice. Nonetheless, it would be disingenuous to claim that there is no overlap between libertarianism and white nationalism.

As an individualist movement, libertarianism is inherently hostile to identity politics. That is, it rejects the idea that the government can make just distinctions between people based on their demographic characteristics. This means that libertarians oppose government-sanctioned discrimination, such as seen in the Jim Crow South, but they also oppose affirmative action, at least when practiced by the government. The libertarian insistence on the sanctity of property rights also leads to their rejection of the Civil Rights Act and other state-led efforts to end private discrimination on the part of businesses. Libertarianism can thus be useful for people who wish to push back against government efforts to promote racial equality but do not wish to be branded as racist. I should again reiterate that I am not claiming that these attitudes are typical among contemporary libertarians. However, it is indisputable that some libertarians have sought to harness white anxieties and use them to further their own cause.

### Who Was Murray Rothbard?

The libertarian strategy of appealing to white frustration is primarily associated with the economist Murray Rothbard, who was one of the best-known promoters of right-wing anarchism in the United States. Rothbard had a long and curious career in political activism. Throughout his life, he was eager to build alliances with any group that hated the U.S. government, especially those that opposed American military force abroad. In the 1930s and 1940s, he made common cause with the so-called Old Right—those right-wing thinkers who preceded the birth of the contemporary conservative movement, and who opposed both the New Deal and American involvement in World War II.

Rothbard showed little interest in the conservative movement, mostly because of its belligerence in the Cold War. In the 1960s, he flirted with activist groups on the New Left, as well as militant groups like the Black Panthers that opposed American imperialism. He hoped that these groups could be persuaded to abandon Marxism in favor of the libertarian position. He eventually gave up on building bridges to the left, which he concluded would never embrace libertarian economics.

In the 1970s, Rothbard helped found the Cato Institute, which is now the most important libertarian think tank in the world. Rothbard broke with Cato after a few years when he determined that it was insufficiently radical. He later played an important role in the Ludwig von Mises Institute, which was more aligned with his political views and preferred economic methods.

In the 1980s, Rothbard turned to the frustrated paleoconservative movement for allies. He hoped that libertarians and paleoconservatives could form a new coalition capable of challenging the mainstream political consensus. Rothbard was enthusiastic about Pat Buchanan's presidential campaign, despite Buchanan's lack of libertarian principles. Buchanan excited Rothbard because of his "America first" foreign policy; Rothbard always viewed noninterventionist foreign policies as critical to the libertarian project.

By the 1990s, Rothbard viewed frustrated whites as a potentially useful ally against big government. He and his allies were willing to accept ideas such as strong immigration restrictions to expand their audience. They also pushed for libertarians to shed their image as part of the counterculture and instead acknowledge the importance of cultural cohesion and homogeneity as a bulwark against a centralizing state. He also defended *The Bell Curve*, the controversial book by Charles Murray and Richard Hernnstein, which argued that IQ differences between racial groups explain some disparities in American life (see the section "What Is Race Realism?" later in this chapter). Rothbard defended the work by noting that it will be helpful for libertarians if they can show that racial disparities are caused by biology rather than systematic discrimination. If these differences are "natural," then it will be more difficult to argue that government must intervene to alleviate them.

Rothbard died in 1994, long before the Alt-Right was born, but many people in the Alt-Right express admiration for Rothbard and his work.

### Who Is Hans-Hermann Hoppe?

Hans-Hermann Hoppe arguably influenced the Alt-Right more than any other libertarian. Hoppe was Murray Rothbard's colleague. He has applied methods developed by the Austrian school of economics to questions about governance, arguing that democracy is possibly the worst of all possible forms of government because of the incentives that it provides leaders. According to Hoppe's book, *Democracy: The God That Failed*, democracies necessarily lead to shortsighted thinking. Although he is an anarchist, he says that if one must have a government, it is better if that government operates as a hereditary monarchy.

Unlike many libertarians, Hoppe does not claim that his brand of libertarianism will lead to a more egalitarian future. He attacks large-scale immigration as a form of forced integration, used by elites to break down traditional forms of solidarity. In his vision of a stateless world, small-scale communities will be ruthless in driving out people who advance dangerous ideas—such as communism, democracy, and egalitarianism.

Hoppe has also been on friendly terms with many people associated with the Alt-Right. He hosts a regular conference in Turkey for his group, called the Property and Freedom Society. Both Richard Spencer and Jared Taylor have addressed this conference. In a 2017 speech, Hoppe gave some qualified praise for the Alt-Right, though he expressed disappointment with its statism and single-minded focus on whiteness.[8]

Although Hoppe is a well-known figure in libertarianism and has been associated with prominent libertarian organizations such as the Ludwig von Mises Institute, he has faced increasing attacks from more mainstream libertarians, who wish to put greater distance between themselves and the Alt-Right.

## What Was the Progressive Movement of the Late Nineteenth and Early Twentieth Centuries?

The ideas promoted by so-called race realists are not new. The notion that racial groups have different cognitive attributes and typical behaviors is centuries old. Thomas Jefferson wrote on this subject, for example. However, the ideas promoted by scientific racists in the Progressive era are the most obvious intellectual antecedents of this element of the Alt-Right.

Many ideas promoted by intellectuals during the Progressive era (which lasted approximately from the 1890s until the 1920s) remain celebrated today. Progressives favored women's suffrage, improved education policies, and fought government corruption. They also led the new conservation movement. Progressives argued that they could improve society by taking a scientific approach to policy.

There was a darker side to the Progressive era, however. Embracing theories promoted by Francis Galton, many Progressives believed genetic differences explained why some population groups exhibited antisocial attributes. They thus applied the same kind of scientific thinking to population policy that they applied to other aspects of government. The eugenics movement sought to encourage supposedly superior people to breed in greater numbers, whereas other parts of the population were discouraged from having children, or even sterilized.

Madison Grant and Lothrop Stoddard were among the most significant figures of the American eugenics movement. Grant was renowned as an intellectual and played an important role in policy debates at that time. He is best known for his 1916 book, *The Passing of the Great Race*. Stoddard, Grant's protégé, published books with even more provocative titles, such as *The Rising Tide of Color Against White World Supremacy* (1920) and *The Revolt Against Civilization* (1922).

The immigration restriction movement had many motivations, but the belief that certain racial and ethnic groups were naturally inferior and thus could not be assimilated was one of the dominant justifications. These ideas had major policy consequences, as the new quota immigration system that was established in the 1920s ushered in a forty-year period of minimal immigration to the United States. Eugenic ideas that originated in the United States also had consequences abroad. The eugenics programs that the Nazis established were modeled on those developed in America, and Hitler expressed his admiration for Madison Grant. These ideas remained commonplace in the United States for many decades. It was not until the aftermath of World War II, when the atrocities committed during that conflict became widely known, that these views became anathema in American social science.

Although the Alt-Right and other white nationalist movements speak fondly of the eugenics movement, these contemporary movements approach the subject somewhat differently. Today's racist extremists usually call for white solidarity across ethnic boundaries. The Progressive eugenicists had a much narrower view of what constituted a "superior" race. Writers such as Grant typically divided Europeans into multiple categories—Grant's classification scheme included "Nordics," "Alpines," and "Mediterraneans." According to these earlier eugenicists, various European groups also possessed different levels of intelligence and agreeableness. In their view, Nordics were unquestionably the superior white race, and the United States should take steps to ensure that they remained the dominant demographic group. For an introduction to eugenicist thought in early twentieth-century America, I recommend Jonathan Peter Spiro's book, *Defending the Master Race: Conservation, Eugenics, and the Legacy of Madison Grant.*

Although the Progressive eugenicists were unquestionably racist and regularly expressed contempt for Africans and Asians, the supposed inferiority of eastern and southern Europeans was among their primary concerns. The immigration quota system that they established was largely aimed to stop the flow of Italian, Polish, and other European immigrants. Within the Alt-Right and similar movements, one can still find people who emphasize these distinctions between European ethnicities. Overall, however, the Alt-Right seeks to foster a pan-European racial identity, which includes white Americans from all European backgrounds.

### What Is Race Realism?

Race realism is a vital component of what I have called highbrow white nationalism. Its proponents view race as a legitimate biological category, rejecting the mainstream consensus that race is a social construct. It holds that various racial groups differ in nonsuperficial ways, though race realists are often particularly obsessed with the subject of IQ.

The idea of racial differences in IQ has long been a common theme in white nationalist discourse, though it became a major topic of national discussion following the 1994 publication of *The Bell Curve* by Charles Murray and Richard Herrnstein. That book argued that IQ was a predictor of economic success, that it was largely hereditary, and that different racial groups had different average IQs. The book was controversial, and many scholars and journalists published lengthy books and articles challenging its conclusions. It remains influential on the radical right, though Murray is not a white nationalist—he describes himself as a libertarian.

Race realism can be viewed as a revival of the scientific racism that was prevalent in the United States during the Progressive era, which promoted state-sponsored eugenics programs and opposed mass immigration, especially from countries outside of Northern Europe. Another common term for race realism is *human biodiversity*, usually shortened to *HBD*, which is a term popularized by the blogger Steve Sailer.

Few contemporary academics espouse these kinds of ideas. Richard Lynn, an emeritus professor at the University of

Ulster, is perhaps the best-known academic promoter of these theories. Lynn argues that different nations have different average IQs, and that these differences are based on genetics. He was an early promoter of the idea that the highest IQs are found in Northeast Asia, and the lowest in sub-Saharan Africa, and that a nation's average IQ score is a powerful predictor of other variables, such as gross domestic product (GDP), fertility, and religiosity. He has also written two books on eugenics, arguing that modern humans are deteriorating in terms of intelligence and health. According to Lynn, this is because modern medicine allows people with major health problems to survive and reproduce, and because modern contraception is used at different rates by people with different characteristics; he argued that intelligent and conscientious people were more likely to control their fertility, limiting their number of offspring compared to other people.

Arthur Jensen, who taught at the University of California, Berkeley, was another well-known promoter of these ideas. Virginia Abernathy, an emeritus professor at Vanderbilt University, has made similar arguments in academic settings. In recent years, Abernathy has been more openly involved in right-wing politics. In 2012, she was the vice-presidential candidate for the white nationalist American Third Position Party, which has since changed its name to the American Freedom Party.

### What Is the Men's Rights Movement?

The Men's Rights Movement (MRM), whose followers are usually described as Men's Rights Advocates (MRAs), is an antifeminist movement that argues that contemporary society discriminates against men in favor of women. For example, it argues that laws regarding child custody and divorce are overtly discriminatory. It similarly argues that, according to many statistics, men are objectively worse off than women in many ways—women live longer, on average, and men are more likely to commit suicide.

Although the MRM has brought up genuine concerns about gender equity, it has often been accused of misogyny. Many voices in the movement go beyond arguing that men suffer systematic discrimination, expressing open contempt for feminism and women more broadly. Like the Alt-Right, the MRM is mostly organized online and contains a network of blogs sometimes called the "manosphere." Within this loose network, one finds many different approaches to gender relations. So-called pick-up artist sites have a wide audience—though these are not always political. These bloggers provide advice on how to seduce women. There is also a more radical antifeminist movement known as Men Going Their Own Way. This group says that feminism has made relations between the sexes so poisonous that heterosexual men should avoid romantic relationships with women entirely, and instead seek sexual satisfaction via prostitution or simply accept celibacy.

It was the MRM that first popularized the "red pill" meme that has since been adopted by the Alt-Right (see the section "What Is the *Red Pill*?" in chapter 5). Much of the Alt-Right holds views on sex and gender relations that are aligned with those of the MRM. The MRM is not inherently racist, and being sympathetic to the MRM does not necessarily suggest that someone agrees with the Alt-Right.

Like the Alt-Right, much of the MRM endorses what is called *sex realism*. This is the idea that men and women have different cognitive characteristics, which are rooted in biology rather than socialization. Because of these different attributes, according to this theory, men and women are biologically suited for different roles in society, and efforts to create higher levels of equality between the sexes will ultimately leave both men and women less happy than they would be under a more traditional, patriarchal system.

### What Was Gamergate?

Gamergate was a controversy that erupted in 2014. When it began, it was purportedly about ethics in video game journalism. It started when a text-based video game created by a developer named Zoe Quinn began to receive positive reviews. Quinn's former romantic partner subsequently accused her of trading sexual favors in exchange for those reviews. This accusation led to a massive backlash from the gaming community, and Quinn was subjected to a harassment campaign that was coordinated on various online forums. The campaign included doxing and death threats.

Gamergate extended beyond the harassment of individuals. The people involved began complaining to advertisers, successfully lobbying some of them to withdraw their support from certain publications. Several people who later became associated with the Alt-Right or Alt-Lite promoted Gamergate, such as Milo Yiannopoulos, Mike Cernovich, and Vox Day.

Gamergate was mostly disconnected from questions of race. Most mainstream commentary on the subject discussed how it revealed troubling misogyny in the gaming community, as well as on the Internet more generally. Supporters of Gamergate were livid that so-called social justice warriors were trying to gain a foothold in the gaming world and institute political correctness in an arena that had previously been mostly free from progressive politics.

In substance, Gamergate did little to directly advance the Alt-Right's agenda. However, it was an early and conclusive demonstration that online trolls (see the section "What Is a Troll?" in chapter 5) could have a substantive influence in the real world. Agitated and persistent trolls caused significant harm to major media institutions. Their attacks helped shut down the major webzine *Gawker*. Despite being a mostly anonymous online mob, the Gamergaters gained the attention of the most important media venues in the United States. Although most Gamergate supporters may not have been white nationalists, the Alt-Right learned from their experience, and many subsequent Alt-Right campaigns utilized similar tactics.

# 5

# THE ALT-RIGHT AND
# THE INTERNET

## *Why Is the Internet So Important to White Nationalists?*

The Internet is a valuable tool for anyone who wants to spread a message to a large audience quickly and inexpensively. It allows easy communication and coordination across diverse groups. A group or individual operating a single website may have difficulty building an audience, but by regularly linking to each other, different sites can amplify each other's reach. The Internet can also be an effective recruiting tool, and this is especially important for radical groups with limited resources. Before the Internet was created, recruitment for extremist groups usually had to take place face to face. The Internet can quietly radicalize people who may never meet an extremist ideologue in real life. Websites that promote far-right ideas but do not present themselves as extremist can be especially useful tools for influencing readers. Sites that downplay extremist rhetoric and avoid hateful slurs often serve as bridges between mainstream and far-right ideologies.

The Alt-Right developed some new methods of using the Internet. However, we should not overstate the degree to which the Alt-Right is qualitatively different from its precursors. The media often presents the Alt-Right as unusually tech savvy. In truth, white nationalists have always been active on the Internet, and they have used it as one of their most important tools since it was created. Tom Metzger (see the section "Who Is Tom Metzger?" in chapter 2), leader of the White Aryan Resistance (WAR), created a computer message board in the 1980s, before most people had even heard of the Internet.

### What Is Stormfront?

Stormfront is the most notorious white nationalist message board. Don Black, a former Ku Klux Klan (KKK) leader and associate of David Duke, created the site in 1995. The site hosts Black's radio show, but it is primarily used as a message board where white nationalists discuss various topics—not all of which are related to race and politics. The site's motto is "White Pride Worldwide," and it has several forums in foreign languages.

Over time, the site became extraordinarily popular, eventually attracting tens of thousands of active posters, and far more monthly page views. Stormfront faced a setback in 2017, when the site's registrar seized its domain name— this was part of the larger wave of digital no-platforming that occurred after the "Unite the Right" rally. Stormfront was back online only a month later, when it found a new provider.

Although Stormfront was created over a decade before the Alt-Right concept was born, the ideological overlap between Stormfront and the rest of the Alt-Right is transparent, and many people who identify with the Alt-Right also post at Stormfront and read its forums. Nonetheless, it does not appear that Stormfront was where most Alt-Right supporters developed their ideas. Far more people in the Alt-Right cite image boards like 4chan (see the section "What Is 4chan?" later in this chapter) as the place where they initially developed their ideas.

### Who Was Bob Whitaker, and What Is "the Mantra"?

Bob Whitaker, a white nationalist propagandist, organized one of the earliest and most effective right-wing online trolling campaigns. Before becoming an open racist agitator, Whitaker worked in mainstream conservative politics. He was an economics professor later appointed by Ronald Reagan to a position in the Office of Personnel Management. Toward the end of his life, he promoted the idea that white nationalist propagandists needed to push their message into mainstream spaces. He created a website called *Bob's Underground Graduate Semininar (B.U.G.S.)*, and his followers are sometimes called *bugsers*.

In 2006, Whitaker created "the Mantra," which makes the case that whites are being victimized by a slow campaign of genocide. It argues that those who campaign for multiculturalism and tolerance are promoting an antiwhite agenda. The mantra ends with the words, "Antiracist is code for antiwhite."

Whitaker's followers have since posted the Mantra, or some variant of it, all across the Internet. When an online news venue that contains a comment section posts a story about race, white nationalists swarm the comments and post the Mantra or some variation of the same idea. At its peak, this effort resulted in the Mantra being posted thousands of times a month.

This was an early example of what the Alt-Right would later call *meme warfare* (see the section "What Is a Meme?" later in this chapter). The constant barrage of white nationalist propaganda was one reason why many news sources changed their policies regarding comments. Many implemented a moderation system, others stopped allowing anonymous comments, and some removed their comment sections entirely.

### What Is a Troll?

A *troll* is a person who provokes discord on the Internet. Trolling does not necessarily serve a greater purpose than the troll's personal amusement. It can take the form of deception, pointless contrarianism, or offensive language. Trolling is common on Internet message boards and social media. Trolls typically operate alone, with little planning ahead of time, though they can also cooperate, either spontaneously or via a planned effort. Trolling is not necessarily political, and when it is political, it is not necessarily right-wing.

### Why Does the Alt-Right Troll?

Although trolling does not necessarily serve a higher purpose than nihilistic amusement, the Alt-Right views it as a serious project. The Alt-Right seeks to disrupt the political and social status quo, and thus takes advantage of every opportunity to sow animosity and distrust. Enraging a political opponent is considered a victory, even if the troll does not change the target's mind about anything. Public trolling on social media or a message board will be viewed by many people not part of the discussion, and these people are often the troll's intended audience.

The Alt-Right wants to discredit mainstream sources of information. Encouraging journalists to pursue fake stories is one of their methods. During the 2016 presidential election, Alt-Right supporters pulled off a number of these pranks, waiting until a story's publication before revealing that they had offered a journalist misleading information. More recently, the Alt-Right promoted the idea that the "okay" hand gesture was a secret code for "White Power" (because three fingers form a "W" and the index finger, thumb, and forearm combine to form a "P"). Many news sources then reported on this, at which point others in the Alt-Right noted that this was untrue.

Right-wing trolls also create and spread memes designed to discredit the left. That is, they start and spread rumors that a left-wing group or individual is promoting a particularly outrageous idea. For example, during the 2016 presidential election cycle, Alt-Right supporters began circulating phony

Clinton campaign material that suggested Hillary Clinton wanted to start a war with Russia and that she wanted women to serve on the front lines of that conflict. Other pranks included trying to get certain hashtags to trend on social media, such as #EndFathersDay and #WhitesCantBeRaped.[1] These kinds of operations are designed to create hostility toward liberals by suggesting that the left is full of people driven by blind hatred for men and white people. These efforts occasionally go viral and can earn tens of thousands of mentions on Twitter in a single day.

Trolls often couch their outrageous racism and anti-Semitism with a layer of irony, creating plausible deniability that they are serious. The combination of extremist imagery and rhetoric with ridiculous humor can confuse outside observers, and when these observers respond with outrage, the troll can respond that it is all just a joke. To some of these trolls, it really is just a joke. To others, breaking down taboos is an important goal.

It is difficult to combat online trolls effectively. A troll views any form of attention—even if it is negative—as a victory. Part of trolling's allure is that it allows anyone, including teenagers at their parents' computers, to have an impact on public debates. Many public figures have adopted the motto, "Don't feed the trolls." However, to ignore them entirely means ceding public spaces on the Internet to the most irresponsible voices.

### What Is a Meme?

A *meme* is just an idea that "goes viral," being absorbed by a large segment of the population. The concept was first popularized by Richard Dawkins in his 1976 book *The Selfish Gene*. A meme is not necessarily political. In fact, most Internet memes are harmless, even nonsensical. They can take the form of a catchphrase, image, hashtag, or video. A successful meme spreads from user to user, and the most successful become permanent fixtures of the Internet. The most well-known Internet memes are usually image macros, in which bolded text surrounds a well-known picture. Some memes develop organically and by chance. Others are the result of a deliberate effort on the part of marketers, political movements, or just individuals who want to spread a message that they consider amusing or important.

### How Does the Alt-Right Use Memes?

The Alt-Right wants to force its ideas into general circulation. Whereas earlier white nationalist content was easy to access online, it was mostly relegated to explicitly racist websites. Because explicit racism was largely cordoned off from the rest of the Internet, it had a limited ability to shape minds. The Alt-Right wants its ideas to penetrate mainstream discourse. Its long-term goal is to normalize the entirety of its ideology. In the short term, it can introduce certain ideas and concepts, with the hope that "normies" (see the section "What Is a Normie, and How Does the Alt-Right Apply the Term?" later in this chapter) will notice and spread them.

The Alt-Right tends to employ two general kinds of memes on social media. The first uses the most shocking language and images possible, such as memes that include jokes about the Holocaust. These memes rarely go viral outside of Alt-Right circles, for understandable reasons. However, by bombarding Internet users with this kind of material, the thinking goes, the Alt-Right weakens its power. Since World War II, the Holocaust has been regularly invoked as a critical moment in history, one that provides important lessons. Throughout the Western world, people learn to be on guard against any kind of policy proposal or cultural trend that is reminiscent of Nazi Germany. The phrase "Never again" has become a fixture of political dialogue in the United States and Europe. This presents a problem for the Alt-Right and related groups. Although most people in the Alt-Right may not endorse anything as extreme as genocide, the policies that many of them do support, such as so-called peaceful ethnic cleansing, remain completely taboo.

To defeat this taboo, the Alt-Right takes a different approach to historical atrocities committed by right-wing movements. Following World War II, many white nationalists and anti-Semites argued that either the Holocaust did not happen, or it was exaggerated. Within the Alt-Right, one still finds these kinds of arguments. Others in the movement, however, have chosen a different rhetorical strategy. Rather than defend the perpetrators of atrocities or claim that these events did not occur, the Alt-Right instead treats them as a joke. The memories of the Holocaust, slavery, and the massacres of indigenous peoples in North America still have important cultural power, and regular reminders of these terrible events are meant to remove some policies and rhetoric permanently from the political discussion. The Alt-Right wants to change this. By making jokes about this material, the online extreme right wants to change how people think about these historical facts. When people think about the Holocaust or slavery, the Alt-Right wants them to remember a funny meme that they recently saw, rather than horrible and disturbing images.

The second category of successful Alt-Right meme is subtler. These memes are not necessarily racist. In fact, they may seem innocuous. Because they seem so harmless, people not affiliated with the Alt-Right may share them. These memes are particularly successful if they provoke a reaction from the left.

The most successful Alt-Right meme of this type in 2017 was the phrase, "It's okay to be white." This concept was developed on 4chan, and it led to a flier campaign in which people hung signs bearing the slogan around college campuses and other public places. The logic of the campaign was that whites are a besieged group, and that they do not need to be ashamed of their race. The larger goal of the campaign, however, was to provoke a media reaction.

This campaign was a success. In some cases, people called the police when they saw the fliers. College administrators felt compelled to denounce them when they appeared on campuses. This provoked conservative commentators, such as Tucker Carlson of the Fox News Channel, to proclaim that these reactions prove that the left has an antiwhite agenda.[2]

These kinds of memes present a new kind of challenge. Because white nationalists and neo-Nazis created and promoted them, responsible people felt that they needed to denounce them. However, by denouncing these fliers, they implied that they disagreed with the slogan, and that it was, in fact, not okay to be white. This reaction fed the narrative that whites are an aggrieved minority, despised by the nation's elites. As a result, some whites may have moved closer to the Alt-Right's position.

Although the Alt-Right's most successful memes suggest that the movement is very skilled when it comes to online marketing and propaganda, we should not overstate this point. Very few Alt-Right memes have achieved the same level of success as "It's okay to be white." Far more attempts to make a particular slogan or idea go viral were unsuccessful. However, with thousands of anonymous posters at various forums sharing ideas, it is inevitable that some of them occasionally will strike a chord and receive widespread attention.

### What Is the ((((Echoes)))) Meme?

In their online writings, supporters of the Alt-Right tend to put three parentheses (which they call *echoes*) around Jewish names. It is unclear who first came up with the idea, but it apparently originated at the website *The Right Stuff* (see the section "What Is *The Right Stuff*?" later in this chapter). The idea soon spread to other Alt-Right websites and social media. The meme is intended to call attention to the large number of Jewish people working in the media, academia, and social activism. The anti-Semitic far right has always claimed that Jews wield disproportionate influence over American life. The Alt-Right also argued that Jewish people are not always up front about their ethno-religious heritage, instead presenting themselves as white Gentiles. By pointing out that an antiracist is

Jewish, the Alt-Right hopes to spread the idea that Jews are opposed to white interests.

As a response to this meme, some Jewish people (and even some non-Jewish people) have begun putting parentheses around their own names as an act of defiance. However, the Alt-Right also considers this a victory, as it further spreads the meme and, in their view, does their work for them. This is another Alt-Right meme that is difficult to combat effectively.

### What Is the Red Pill?

The *red pill* is a reference to *The Matrix*, a 1999 science-fiction film. In the film, the protagonist is given a choice between learning the true nature of reality (by "taking the red pill") or remaining ignorant of truths that the world's malevolent overlords keep hidden from most people ("taking the blue pill"). Had the character chosen the blue pill, he would have returned to his life of relative ease and comfort, but he would remain forever unaware of deeper truths. Taking the red pill, in contrast, leads to a meaningful life, but also one of constant danger and challenge.

As is the case with other memes, the red pill metaphor did not originate from the Alt-Right. It was first popularized by the Men's Rights Movement (MRM), which opposes feminism and argues that gender egalitarianism is based on falsehoods that harm men (see the section "What Is the Men's Rights Movement?" in chapter 4). A documentary called *The Red Pill*, which was about the MRM, was released in 2015. Although the Alt-Right and the MRM are not synonymous, there is significant overlap, and most of the Alt-Right agrees with Men's Rights Advocates (MRAs) on questions of gender relations.

Within the Alt-Right, *the red pill* usually refers to racial differences and Jewish influence on American society. According to the Alt-Right, most Americans are so immersed in egalitarian thinking that they cannot comprehend truths that are right in front of them. Within Alt-Right venues, one regularly finds stories of people describing their red-pill experience.

Congruent with the plot of *The Matrix*, people in the Alt-Right describe the red pill as liberating, but also the source of many difficulties. Some people within the movement have described how their new beliefs make social situations awkward in a way they were not before. Others note that the red pill instills a powerful urge to act on their new beliefs and spread their ideas as widely as possible.

Over time, the Alt-Right also began using colored pills to describe all sorts of information. "White pills" reference news that is good for the movement; "black pills" are stories or ideas that the Alt-Right finds depressing.

## What Is Pepe the Frog?

The Alt-Right adopted Pepe as a mascot of sorts. Pepe is an anthropomorphic frog. The character first originated as part of a comic strip on the social media platform MySpace in 2005. Although Pepe was often depicted engaging in vulgar behavior, there was nothing inherently racist about the character. He eventually became popular on 4chan, 8chan, and Reddit. For a time, even after his popularity grew, Pepe was not necessarily associated with racism, and several notable celebrities were sharing Pepe images as recently as 2014.

Over time, however, Pepe became increasingly popular with the far right online. In 2015, Donald Trump was depicted as Pepe on Twitter, and Trump himself retweeted the image. Pepe became increasingly depicted in a transparently racist or anti-Semitic context. For example, it is easy to find images of the frog dressed in a Nazi uniform.

Pepe became so associated with the Alt-Right that a number of high-profile venues decided to publish pieces explaining that the meme was no longer harmless, and that the people who use it may be pushing a darker agenda. In 2016, the Hillary Clinton campaign posted a page on its website explaining and denouncing Pepe. The Anti-Defamation League (ADL) also included an entry about Pepe in the category of general hate symbols—though the entry made it clear that because the image is not inherently racist, one should be cautious before denouncing someone for sharing a Pepe image.

As 2016 progressed, elements of the Alt-Right created a bizarre backstory for Pepe, stating that he is the latest incarnation of the Egyptian god Kek. Alt-Right circles began talking about "Esoteric Kekism" as their religion. White nationalists in the past have tried to create and promote their own religious cults, such as Cosmotheism, the Christian Identity Movement, and the Creativity Movement. Kekism is qualitatively different from these earlier cases, however. I am aware of no one in the Alt-Right who earnestly promotes this religious concept. It is instead treated as an elaborate inside joke, yet another way the Alt-Right seeks to baffle outsiders.

Pepe has raised additional, broader questions about intellectual property in the Internet age. Although Pepe was first created by a cartoonist named Matt Furie—who is not a racist—the most iconic Pepe images were created by other people, most of whom are anonymous posters on Internet forums. Furie reached out to the Anti-Defamation League to reclaim Pepe from the Alt-Right.[3] Furie's attorneys also sought to block others from profiting from the use of Pepe. Most notably, these attorneys successfully blocked many Alt-Right authors from publishing books with Pepe on the cover. In addition, Furie's attorneys demanded that figures such as Richard Spencer and Mike Cernovich stop using Pepe's image on their Web platforms.

These legal threats did not stop Twitter users and posters at anonymous forums from using Pepe's image. A similar character named "Groyper," described in *Slate* as a "fatter, more racist Pepe the frog,"[4] is now also popular with the Alt-Right.

Many people remain mystified as to how an innocuous cartoon frog with no ideological content became associated with white nationalism and anti-Semitism. The reality is that there was, to the best of my knowledge, no planning involved in this development. Using the image in a racist context amused some early Alt-Right supporters, and others agreed that it was humorous. Its use of nonsensical imagery also shows the degree to which the Alt-Right is ensconced in the broader Internet culture. Mystifying lingo and images are a barrier to entry for people trying to make sense of a group or movement. Pepe is also useful to the Alt-Right because he is a disarming character. Rather than burning crosses or pictures from Nuremberg rallies, many people in the Alt-Right used a harmless cartoon frog as their symbol, making it less clear if the movement was truly committed to an ideology or if it was just engaged in an elaborate prank or an apolitical trolling campaign.

It is significant that the most important Alt-Right venues used Pepe less frequently after 2016. Lawsuit threats may have been one major catalyst for this, but it may signify something more important. In 2017, there was a serious push to take the Alt-Right into the real world. This meant adopting a new tone and style, as aesthetic sensibilities of Internet message boards do not translate well into real-world rallies and protests. Much of the Alt-Right has dropped the irony and humor that characterized the movement in 2015 and 2016.

### What Is a Normie, and How Does the Alt-Right Apply the Term?

The Alt-Right regularly uses the term *normie*, though it did not originate with the movement. Broadly speaking, a normie, in Internet slang, is someone conventional and not a part of an online subculture, who does not get what the group is fundamentally about. The Alt-Right typically applies the term to white people who are not "racially aware." In this context, a normie is someone who generally supports mainstream politics and finds racism distasteful. The Alt-Right does not identify normies as their primary enemy. Many debates within the Alt-Right center on how they should frame their arguments to appeal to the greatest number of normies. That is, some in the Alt-Right argue that the most extreme rhetoric and images (swastikas, for example) are off-putting to most white Americans and thus should be avoided. Others argue that normies, who will maintain their bourgeois mindset and never embrace radical ideas, are not the movement's target audience, so alienating them does not matter.

### What Is 4chan?

The 4chan site is an online image board that Christopher Poole created in 2003. It allows users to post content anonymously. It was described in *The New York Times* as "one of the darkest corners of the Web."[5] Although elements of the Alt-Right congregate on 4chan and related sites, its creator did not intend the site to be a source of racist content, nor was that what it was primarily known for during most of its history. Even today, 4chan is not predominantly a racist website—though one can find offensive material on most of its boards.

The format of 4chan is not unique. It is divided into various topics, and within each topic, the most recent comments appear first. It is notable because of its anonymous nature (one does not need to register or provide a user name when posting on 4chan) and because it has a massive audience. The site has millions of monthly visitors. It is difficult to study systematically, both because the people who post there are anonymous and because it does not maintain a permanent archive and most threads expire quickly. Further, 4chan and similar sites are even more perplexing to many outside observers because they maintain a distinct lingo and no glossary to help new users orient themselves. More experienced posters often mock new users who demonstrate a lack of familiarity with a board's terms and culture. New readers of the site are encouraged to "lurk more" before contributing.

Most of the boards on 4chan are not political. They include boards dedicated to some element of pop culture, pornography, fitness, or technology. The most notorious element of 4chan, however, is /pol/, which stands for "politically incorrect." First created in 2011, this discussion board quickly became the most aggressively racist element of 4chan. At all times, the page is filled with Nazi imagery and racial slurs. In addition, it is where many Alt-Right memes and trolling campaigns begin. The site 8chan also has an image board called /pol/, which includes similar content.

Although appalling content of many varieties can be found on 4chan, the site does have rules. Illegal material is prohibited on all boards. Doxing is also not permitted. Within 4chan, different boards have their own rules, banning racism, pornography, and other offensive material. Others have very few rules. Aside from /pol/, the most infamous board on 4chan is /b/, the "random" board, which has no rules of its own and only enforces the global 4chan rules.

The political elements of 4chan are not exclusively right-wing. A 4chan user, for example, hacked former Alaska governor Sarah Palin's email, hoping to find embarrassing information—but he apparently failed to find anything interesting.[6] Left-wing 4chan trolls were also associated with online attacks on the Church of Scientology, as well as on the white supremacist radio host Hal Turner.[7]

For a useful introduction to chan culture and its role in the Alt-Right, I recommend Angela Nagle's book, *Kill All Normies*. For a broader discussion of 4chan's early history, I recommend Cole Stryker's book, *Epic Win for Anonymous*.

### What Is Twitter, and Why Is It Useful to the Alt-Right?

Although Alt-Right content is usually generated at explicitly racist websites and image boards, Twitter is the Alt-Right's most effective means of circulating these ideas and images. It is a social media platform where people have a limited number of characters (originally 140, but now 280) to express a thought. Most content posted on Twitter is not racist or even political, but it can be a useful tool for online propagandists. Alt-Right content is also present on other social media sites, but Twitter offers many advantages to radical movements. It allows the use of anonymous accounts, unlike Facebook, which requires users to provide their names. One only needs an e-mail address to join Twitter, which means one person can operate multiple accounts on Twitter by just having several e-mail addresses.

Twitter also makes it easy to engage strangers in a conversation. On Facebook, interactions occur primarily between "friends." On Twitter, you can tag people in tweets or comment on their tweets, even if they do not follow you. It is possible to block specific users from engaging with your account, but the ease with which a person can generate a new Twitter account makes this a minor inconvenience.

Twitter is important because a massive number of public figures use the site—President Trump, for example. Public figures often have a blue check mark attached to their profile to verify their identity and distinguish them from potential impersonators. The site is a valuable tool for politicians, journalists, and celebrities who want to disseminate a message to their followers quickly. However, the site also allows anyone to respond to these messages. The person who made the original post and anyone who clicks on the tweet is then able to see the responses. Unlike comment sections on online news stories, there is no process for filtering responses and mentions on Twitter—though, as mentioned, people can block specific accounts from interacting with them.

This was the initial means by which the Alt-Right first came to major public attention. At the start of 2015, the number of people who identified as Alt-Right was small. However, they steadily built up a presence on Twitter and began to harass many public figures relentlessly, responding to their tweets with racist and anti-Semitic invective.

By engaging with these public figures, the Alt-Right could spread its message to a new, previously inaccessible audience. Important public figures often enjoy millions of Twitter followers, far more than even the most well-known figures in the Alt-Right. By replying to tweets from prominent people, they can ensure that a massive number of people view their message. Trolls are especially delighted when the targeted person interacts with them, even to denounce them. Such interactions demonstrate that the troll provoked an emotional response, and the interaction also brings the troll a much larger number of views. Once someone has engaged with a troll, other trolls are likely to join the conversation in the hope of continuing the discussion and gaining additional attention.

Alt-Right trolls also monitor the social media activity of important people. If a prominent person on Twitter makes a remark that can be reasonably viewed as an attack on white people, the Alt-Right will quickly retweet the comment. This helps them promote the idea that the nation's elites are hostile to whites. Sometimes these Alt-Right supporters are clearly taking a tweet out of context. In other cases, the person genuinely did say something offensive and impolite.

It is possible to delete a tweet, and some people do that when faced with a backlash. However, Alt-Right trolls will often take a screenshot of the tweet, preserving it if it is deleted. The use of screenshots creates an additional challenge for people trying to protect their online reputation. It is easy to use Photoshop or other editing software to change the words in a tweet and then repost it online. These phony tweets can then go viral.

Twitter also makes it easy to create large, private group conversations via direct messages. This allows people in the Alt-Right to communicate with each other without providing any additional information beyond their Twitter handles. A 2018 leak of Twitter direct messages revealed that Alt-Right political candidate Paul Nehlen (see the section "Are There Alt-Right Politicians?" in chapter 6) used this method to enlist online supporters for a trolling campaign.[8]

### How Has Twitter Tried to Limit the Alt-Right's Influence?

From its origins until 2016, Twitter took a mostly hands-off approach to right-wing radicalism on its platform, provided that no one was breaking any laws. As the Alt-Right became increasingly prominent, however, Twitter began to take concerns about harassment and hate speech more seriously. In 2016, Twitter's Trust and Safety Council began to work with experts to find ways to prevent abuse. Twitter's declining patience for right-wing provocation was displayed when the site acted against Milo Yiannopoulos in 2016 (see the section "Who Is Milo Yiannopoulos?" in chapter 9). It first removed his "verified" status, and later banned him from the platform entirely. These actions resulted from Yiannipoulos's attack on Leslie Jones, an African American actor, who subsequently received a barrage of racist and misogynistic insults from Yiannipoulos's followers. Twitter also banned high-profile Alt-Right users such as Ricky Vaughn.

On its face, being banned from Twitter may seem like a minor inconvenience, especially if someone was operating an anonymous account; one can easily create a new anonymous account and return to the platform. However, building up a large following takes time, and a person may never be able to return to his or her original level of influence.

Throughout 2016 and 2017, Twitter continued to remove Alt-Right accounts that violated the site's terms of service. In December 2017, the site stepped up its enforcement even further, removing several accounts simultaneously. Twitter announced the following new rules:

> You may not make specific threats of violence or wish for the serious physical harm, death, or disease of an individual or group of people. This includes, but is not limited to, threatening or promoting terrorism. You also may not affiliate with organizations that—whether by their own statements or activity both on and off the

platform—use or promote violence against civilians to further their causes.[9]

Although these rules seem straightforward, it remains unclear how Twitter discerns when a person has violated them. The new standards were put in place on December 18, and immediately afterward, many significant Alt-Right accounts were suspended. Jared Taylor, Hunter Wallace, and Matt Parrot were suspended, as were the accounts for Identity Evropa, *American Renaissance,* Britain First, and the Traditionalist Worker Party (TWP).

This new crackdown, however, was also confusing, as Twitter did not explain how it determined which accounts it targeted. Jared Taylor is a white nationalist, but his use of the platform did not seem to violate any of its rules. Taylor subsequently announced that he would sue Twitter. Many accounts with more extreme timelines were not targeted, and several prominent Alt-Right accounts were also left in place. Richard Spencer, David Duke, and Mike Enoch remained active. Thus, this so-called purge did little to remove the Alt-Right's presence on Twitter, and the sort of behavior that would result in a ban remained unclear.

### What Are the Most Important Alt-Right Forums?

Historically, Stormfront has been the most influential white nationalist online forum (see the section "What Is Stormfront?" earlier in this chapter). It remains the most heavily trafficked site of its kind. A former National Alliance member named Alex Linder set up a similar site, Vanguard News Network, in 2000. Vanguard News Network is arguably even more extreme than Stormfront. A few other Alt-Right and white nationalist forums have also appeared in recent years. As is the case with Stormfront, these forums primarily discuss racial and political issues, but one can also find general discussions about pop culture and other topics. Different forums have different tones and levels of moderation. For a time, there was a popular Alt-Right subreddit called "r/altright," but it was shut down when its users repeatedly violated Reddit's terms of service. Other popular Alt-Right forums are independent of larger platforms, such as the forum hosted at *The Right Stuff* and forums such as "My Posting Career" and "Salo Forum."

### Who Is Andrew Anglin, and What Is The Daily Stormer?

*The Daily Stormer* was founded by Andrew Anglin. He embraces radical right-wing rhetoric and imagery, openly celebrating Nazi Germany. He was not always a racist activist; he used to write about conspiracy theories. Originally from Ohio, Anglin spent a significant number of time living overseas. His first foray into the world on Internet racism was a short-lived blog called *Total Fascism*, which he eventually abandoned to create *The Daily Stormer* in 2013. Aside from Anglin, the most well known figure associated with the website is a white nationalist troll and hacker who uses the name Weev.

According to its own estimates, *The Daily Stormer* is the most visited Alt-Right website in the world. It is also among the most extreme when it comes to racism and anti-Semitism; it took its name from the Nazi publication *Der Stürmer. The Daily Stormer* is particularly focused on anti-Semitism, insisting that all of the world's major problems can be blamed on Jews. This single-minded focus is deliberate: A leaked document providing guidelines for *Daily Stormer* articles included the following text: "Prime Directive: Always Blame the Jews for Everything."[10]

*The Daily Stormer* is so extreme that it has been criticized by other elements of the Alt-Right, who argue that the site's ostentatious vitriol toward minorities and embrace of Nazi imagery and rhetoric causes harm to the overall movement. Some in the Alt-Right even speculated that "Anglin is a paid shill and agent provocateur, whose purpose is simply to infest and discredit White nationalism."[11] These accusations have mostly stopped, however.

In late 2017, Anglin suggested the Alt-Right should develop a new strategy, at least in its real-world activism. After the "Unite the Right" rally, he began arguing that future Alt-Right events in the real world needed to ditch Nazi imagery and instead embrace the American flag. His website, however, continues to use Nazi symbols and talking points.

Besides the site's outrageous content, *The Daily Stormer* is notorious for the real-world actions taken by some of its readers. A report by the Southern Poverty Law Center suggests that Dylann Roof, who massacred nine African Americans in a church in South Carolina, had posted comments at *The Daily Stormer*.[12] The site is also known for its loosely organized "Stormer Troll Army." These are *Daily Stormer* readers who harass people discussed on the site, writing obscene and threatening e-mails and social media comments.

The most significant of these coordinated harassment efforts occurred in late 2016, when *Daily Stormer* readers began sending threatening and anti-Semitic e-mails, letters, and phone calls to a Montana realtor named Tanya Gersh. Prior to this campaign, Gersh had urged Sherry Spencer (Richard Spencer's mother) to sell property that she owned in Whitefish, Montana, due to her son's reputation. Anglin and others accused Gersh of extortion.

In 2017, *The Daily Stormer* was at the center of a new effort to deplatform the extreme elements of the Alt-Right from the Internet. Following the "Unite the Right" rally, Anglin posted insulting remarks about Heather Heyer, the antiracist protester killed at the event. In response, *The Daily Stormer's* domain registrar announced that it would no longer host the site. Other companies similarly refused to host the website, and for a time, *The Daily Stormer* was accessible only on the so-called Dark Web via the web browser Tor. For the next several months, *The Daily Stormer* attempted to register with multiple domains, most of which were hosted abroad. At the time of this writing, *The Daily Stormer* is back online via a ".name" domain name. By the time this book goes to print, it may be something else.

On his personal blog, which he set up shortly after *The Daily Stormer* was first removed from the Internet, Anglin explained the logic of his persona. He argued that the site and the figure that he presented to the world should be considered "performance art." He noted that by being extreme, he could draw more attention to himself and his ideas than would have been possible otherwise. In this regard, Anglin is like earlier white nationalist agitators like George Lincoln Rockwell.[13]

Compared to other leading figures in the Alt-Right, Anglin is notoriously elusive. Unlike Richard Spencer, Mike Enoch, and other famous people associated with the movement, Anglin rarely gives comments to mainstream journalists. His recent secrecy appears to be, at least in part, due to his efforts to avoid legal trouble. At the time of this writing, Anglin faces a lawsuit from Gersh. The lawsuit is presently hindered, however, by authorities' inability to locate him. He currently claims to live in Nigeria, though there is little evidence for this, and one of the process servers hired to find Anglin believes that he saw him in late 2017 in Ohio.[14]

Anglin is one of the few figures in the Alt-Right who has been able to turn racist activism into a major source of income. He solicits donations via Bitcoin at *The Daily Stormer* and has raised thousands of dollars from the website *Hatreon*.

### What *Is* The Right Stuff?

*The Right Stuff* is one of the most influential websites in the Alt-Right. It grew out of a libertarian discussion group on Facebook, and after it was established as its own website, its contributors continued to post right-wing libertarian material.

Over time, the site moved in a more explicitly white nationalist direction.

Although it publishes essays and maintains a forum, *The Right Stuff* is best known for hosting podcasts. The site's flagship podcast is known as *The Daily Shoah* (*TDS*)—the name is a combination of the *The Daily Show* (the program on Comedy Central) and the Hebrew term used to describe the Holocaust. The show combines racist rhetoric with informal banter that often has no political or racial content. Its main hosts use the pseudonyms Mike Enoch and Seventh Son. Unlike some other Alt-Right podcasts, such as those hosted by Richard Spencer and Jared Taylor, *TDS* has no shortage of racial slurs and other crude language. In terms of content, *TDS* presents a message similar to other white nationalist broadcasts. However, *TDS* differs from its white nationalist predecessors in its tone. *TDS* mimics "shock jock" radio shows such as *Opie and Anthony*. It often presents its racism in a lighthearted and ironic manner, playing racist parody songs, for example. Instead of only broadcasting political tirades, *TDS* attracts listeners by providing entertainment along with its white nationalist message.

*Fash the Nation* (*FTN*) is the other most significant podcast hosted at *The Right Stuff*. Its hosts use the names Jazzhands McFeels and Halberstram. This program provides political and cultural analysis analogous to what one would find on a more mainstream radio network, but from a white nationalist perspective.

Many people associated with *The Right Stuff* were doxed in 2016 (see the section "What Is Doxing?" in chapter 10). Antiracist activists revealed the identities of both Mike Enoch and Seventh Son, as well as many other people associated with the site. This doxing revealed that Enoch's wife was Jewish. As a result, it appeared that *TDS* would lose much of its fan base. After many other people in the movement, such as Richard

Spencer and Andrew Anglin, defended Enoch, the site apparently recovered. No longer hiding his face, Enoch subsequently engaged in real-world activism and began appearing at public events. In 2017, *The Right Stuff* began to raise additional money by creating a paywall on the site, making some content available only to paid subscribers.

# 6

# THE ALT-RIGHT OFFLINE

## Who Funds the Alt-Right?

For the time being, the Alt-Right operates on a shoestring budget. Unlike conservatism, libertarianism, and other more mainstream ideologies, the movement does not possess a deep pool of wealthy benefactors. Nor does it, at this point, have a well-organized system for raising large sums via small donations—though this may be changing.

Throughout the history of American white nationalism, we can find many examples of leading figures who were self-funded. That is, they made their money by other means and then used it to grow their movement. Ben Klassen (see the section "What Is the Church of the Creator?" in chapter 3), for example, had some success in real estate before turning to racist activism.

White nationalist organizations have also tried to stay financially solvent by charging membership fees. This was not a panacea; the modal person drawn to such organizations was not necessarily well off financially, so these dues were either meager or not regularly collected. In addition, white nationalists have funded their groups by selling racist clothing and patches or music with racist lyrics. The National Alliance (see the section "Who Was William Pierce, and What Is the National Alliance?" in chapter 2) ran the record label

Resistance Records. Some money generated by criminal activity also made its way into white nationalist coffers.

The fundraising tactics that earlier white nationalists employed were not particularly effective. However, the Alt-Right may be even more strapped for cash. Although there are now a handful of membership-based organizations, they have a relatively small following. The number of people willing to spend money on racist music also seems to have declined. Some of the more popular Alt-Right websites, such as *The Right Stuff*, have created a paywall that provides additional content to people who are willing to pay extra. It is unclear how much more income this delivers.

William Regnery II is the best-known benefactor of the Alt-Right, though his support for the white nationalist movement precedes the term's creation. The Regnery family has long been a crucial element of the mainstream conservative movement, publishing some of its most influential books and publications. Henry Regnery helped launched *Human Events*, an important conservative magazine, in 1944. Regnery Publishing also published classic texts such as Russell Kirk's book *The Conservative Mind*. Regnery Publishing remains one of the most influential publishers of conservative books, many of which become major best-sellers.

William Regnery II, Henry's nephew, inherited a considerable fortune, and in his early life, he was involved with mainstream conservative groups. Eventually, however, he focused his attention and resources on open white nationalism. He founded the Charles Martel Society in 2001, named for the Frankish military leader who halted the Arab invasion of Western Europe at the Battle of Tours in 732. The Charles Martel Society is best known for its publication, *The Occidental Quarterly*, a white nationalist journal. Regnery also helped create the NPI in 2005.

Although Regnery has played an important role in supporting groups affiliated with the Alt-Right, his contributions should be put in context. He has given six-figure sums to various white nationalist enterprises. A report by *Buzzfeed* calculated that he has given at least $580,000 to white nationalist groups since 2001.[1] Compared to the mainstream right's most generous benefactors, however, this is a small amount. Charles and David Koch (known as "the Koch brothers" for short) alone have donated more than $100 million to their causes, and the nonprofits that they helped create subsequently built their own fundraising apparatuses. Because of these major benefactors, conservatism and libertarianism can claim an army of activists who make their living promoting their cause. The Alt-Right cannot do the same.

The Pioneer Fund is another source of far-right income, though this group focuses on academic work. It has provided funding for right-wing scholars like Arthur Jensen and J. Philip Rushton, though it has also supported Jared Taylor's organization. It has not, to my knowledge, ever provided financial support to Alt-Right activist groups.

Most of the significant online venues for Alt-Right materials hold regular fundraising campaigns, though if the numbers that these websites present are accurate, these appeals rarely (if ever) bring in sums above five figures. The Alt-Right has recently had some success at crowdfunding—raising money off the Internet by requesting small sums from many people. This became more difficult when the major crowdfunding websites, such as Patreon and GoFundMe, started banning Alt-Right groups and individuals in 2017. Because of this challenge, the Alt-Right started creating its own platforms (see the section "What Is Alt-Tech?" in chapter 10). The Alt-Right alternative to Patreon, Hatreon, is a source of funding for some of the major Alt-Right personalities, though it is currently disabled and it is not clear if it will be revived.

Despite these efforts to fund the movement, the Alt-Right can presently sustain only a small number of full-time activists and content creators. Most people affiliated with the Alt-Right are volunteers or receive a small fraction of their income from their activism efforts. This is one of the reasons doxing is such a threat to the Alt-Right. The movement does not have the funds to assist many of the people who lose their ability to make a living after their activism is exposed. According to the Anti-Defamation League (ADL), "Because of the comparatively small size of the white supremacist movement and the relative lack of wealth within it, the movement is limited in the amount of money that it can generate."[2]

This lack of funding places severe limits on what the Alt-Right can accomplish offline. Some Alt-Right groups have developed strategies for community outreach and recruitment, but they have not been effectively implemented because of their lack of resources. For example, Matthew Heimbach's group, the Traditionalist Worker Party (TWP) (see the section "Who Is Matthew Heimbach, and What Was the Traditionalist Worker Party?" later in this chapter), said that it wanted to model itself on groups like Hezbollah and the Irish Republican Army (IRA). Although these groups are best known for their terrorist activities, they also provided resources to people in their local communities, earning trust and support. Even if Heimbach's plan was sound in theory, however, TWP did not have the funds to follow through on this plan. Hezbollah receives significant sums from the Iranian government, and the IRA at its peak had a powerful international fundraising operation—raising considerable amounts of money from places such as the United States. No Alt-Right group can make a similar claim.

### What Is the National Policy Institute?

The National Policy Institute (NPI) is the main think tank associated with the Alt-Right, though it was created before the term was coined. William Regnery II and Sam Francis created NPI in 2005. A white nationalist named Louis Andrews led the organization until 2011, when Richard Spencer became its new president. NPI has received funding from Regnery, as well as from the Pioneer Fund. It was organized as a nonprofit organization, but the Internal Revenue Service (IRS) revoked its tax-exempt status in 2017. This decision by the IRS was not apparently motivated by ideology; the group failed to submit the correct paperwork to maintain its status as a 501(c)(3) organization.

Under Spencer's leadership, the group's public profile grew considerably. It regularly publishes reports on questions related to race. Spencer's website, *Radix Journal*, was an NPI initiative. NPI is best known for hosting an annual conference. It was at the now-infamous 2016 NPI conference that Spencer exclaimed "Hail Trump," and some in the audience responded with Nazi salutes.

### What Are the Major Alt-Right Conferences?

Since 1994, Jared Taylor has hosted regular *American Renaissance* conferences. Until 2008, these meetings took place every other year. They can draw several hundred attendees. The first *American Renaissance* conference was broadcast on CSPAN.

The *American Renaissance* conference is a highbrow gathering, with a format analogous to academic conferences. Speakers give a prepared speech, often accompanied with Microsoft PowerPoint slides, and then take questions from the audience. Attendees are expected to follow a dress code and maintain certain standards of civility—racial slurs and calls for violent revolution are notably absent from these conferences.

Some of the most prominent white nationalists, immigration restrictionists, and paleoconservatives in the United States and abroad have addressed *American Renaissance* conferences. Notable speakers have included Sam Francis, Peter Brimelow, Richard Spencer, Guillaume Faye, and Taylor himself.

In 2010, *American Renaissance* faced a new challenge. Taylor had previously held these conferences at privately owned hotels. When the 2010 conference location was revealed, antiracist activists began calling the venue to protest, some even threatening violence, ultimately forcing the event's cancellation. Taylor sought unsuccessfully to find a new location to host the conference, and the event was eventually cancelled altogether. *American Renaissance* was similarly unable to find a venue willing to host the conference in 2011.

Taylor solved this problem by renting a location on government property, such as in a national park. Unlike private businesses, which are free to deny services to groups promoting ideas they dislike, the government must respect every group's First Amendment rights. *American Renaissance* has been able to hold a conference every year since 2012 as a result.

The NPI also hosted several conferences since Richard Spencer took over that organization. These conferences have historically followed a similar format to *American Renaissance* conferences. Like *American Renaissance*, NPI has also recently had trouble finding venues. In previous years, NPI has hosted its conference in the Ronald Reagan Building in Washington, D.C. In 2017, however, the managers denied their request for space, citing security concerns. Spencer subsequently attempted to host a smaller conference on private property but was forced to leave the venue after the owner realized it was a white nationalist event.

Other white nationalist groups also hold occasional meetups. Stormfront, for example, held a summit in Tennessee in 2017.

### Who Is Matthew Heimbach, and What Was the Traditionalist Worker Party?

Matthew Heimbach is one of the main public faces of explicit white nationalism in the United States. He formed a White Student Union at Towson University in 2012 and led the organization until his graduation in 2013. The group was controversial from the beginning. Heimbach and others in the group held campus patrols at night, claiming that minority crime was out of control. They also invited Jared Taylor to give a speech on campus.

Following his graduation, Heimbach cofounded the Traditionalist Youth Network along with a white nationalist named Matthew Parrot. This later became the Traditionalist Worker Party (TWP). Despite the name, partisan politics was not the TWP's primary endeavor, though it has endorsed a handful of unsuccessful candidates for public office and it raised money for this purpose. Public activism and community organizing were their main activities. Unlike most of the Alt-Right, Orthodox Christianity was central to the TWP's ideology—though Heimbach was excommunicated by his church for promoting racism. Although there are other Christians in the Alt-Right, few treat Christianity as a key source of their ideological beliefs.

Heimbach is also distinct for openly courting the radical right's most extreme elements. Early on, he sought to build bridges to the remnants of White Nationalism 1.0 (see chapter 2). He has spoken at a Stormfront conference, reached out to skinhead gangs, and collaborated with the National Socialist Movement (NSM). This made Heimbach controversial among more moderate elements of the Alt-Right, which want to move away from the pageantry and threatening imagery traditionally associated with white nationalism.

Despite building alliances with the most extreme fringes of the radical right, Heimbach tried to avoid expressions of racial hatred in his public statements. He avoided racial slurs and pronouncements of white superiority. Further, the group has sought to build relationships with black nationalists who also want to see the races separated. Although he avoided statements of overt white supremacism, Heimbach and the rest of the TWP were openly anti-Semitic.

TWP was reactionary on questions of race and culture, but it was opposed to conservatism on most other issues. It attacked capitalism and openly described itself as national socialist on economic matters. Its website declared, "Today's global capitalist system is the enemy of all humanity and represents the greatest threat to the continued existence of our people."[3] The group argued that the capitalist elites hate racially aware whites and view them as a threat to their long-term vision for the world. Heimbach has also declared that he hates America.

Although TWP always had an online presence, it emphasized building a real-world movement to a greater degree than most of the Alt-Right. It was particularly active in the Appalachian region of the United States, where a large portion of poor whites live. It aspired to provide services in some of these communities to build goodwill among the locals and eventually swell its ranks.

Heimbach brought several white nationalist groups together under a single banner. The recently formed Nationalist Front held public events including the TWP, the NSM, The League of the South, and Vanguard America. For a thorough discussion of Heimbach's goals and strategies, I recommend *Everything You Love Will Burn*, by Vegas Tenold.

Because of its extreme rhetoric and focus on the real world, I was ambivalent as to whether the TWP should be classified as Alt-Right or White Nationalist 1.0. In many ways, it modeled itself on older white nationalist organizations. I decided to include it here because of the many times that it cooperated with Alt-Right groups and personalities. The question is probably moot at this point. In early 2018, the TWP collapsed because of internal drama within the organization. A domestic dispute involving Heimbach and Parrot ended with Heimbach's arrest for battery. Although Heimbach has not yet been tried, he was on probation at the time that these events allegedly transpired, and he may be imprisoned as a result. Regardless of the legal problems he may face, Heimbach's reputation in the movement is permanently ruined. Parrot stated that he is giving up on activism and deleted the group's website. Although other members of the TWP may attempt to reorganize someday, at present it looks like it is finished as an organization.

### What Is Identity Evropa?

Identity Evropa is a new Alt-Right organization dedicated to real-world activism. Founded in 2016, it is one of the few groups associated with this movement with a formal membership process. Identity Evropa members are required to pay dues but not required to take part in public activism. It has become a major player in real-world Alt-Right activism.

Identity Evropa models itself on the European Identitarian movement (see the section "What Is the Identitarian Movement?" in chapter 3); their website includes a quote from Guillame Faye. It primarily focuses its recruiting efforts on college campuses. Although it has been involved in major Alt-Right rallies—notably the "Unite the Right" rally—it does not typically announce its activities ahead of time. It more frequently engages in "flash mob" tactics, in which members quickly assemble in a location, express their message, and disperse. For example, the group hangs banners with right-wing slogans from freeway overpasses, so motorists below will see them. The group also holds brief protests in public places and hangs fliers around college campuses. Like TWP, Identity Evropa engages in occasional community-service projects to build support.

Identity Evropa avoids the symbols traditionally associated with American white nationalism and neo-Nazism. Its materials do not contain Confederate flags or swastikas. To demonstrate to the public that they are made up of healthy and well-adjusted people, they vet potential members and demand that members "keep themselves in good physical shape and generally present themselves in a professional and positive manner when in public."[4]

Although Identity Evropa has sought to maintain a more professional and clean-cut image than other white nationalist groups, it has been involved in violent protests. The group's former leader, Nathan Damigo, was filmed punching a counterprotester at an event in Berkeley, California, in early

2017. As mentioned, it also helped organize the "Unite the Right" rally.

Since "Unite the Right," and the many schisms that emerged from the Alt-Right, Identity Evropa has suffered a crisis of leadership and direction. Damigo stepped down as head of the organization at the end of August 2017, and was replaced by Eli Mosley. Mosley's tenure as leader of Identity Evropa was also short, and he was replaced by Patrick Casey in December. Following his departure from Identity Evropa, Mosley remained a major player in Alt-Right activism; he continued to collaborate with Richard Spencer and NPI. This ended in February 2018, when a reporter from *The New York Times* published a report showing that Mosley had exaggerated his experience in the U.S. army[5]—much of his public persona was built around the claim that he was a disenchanted combat veteran. According to this report, Mosley had never served in combat or been deployed overseas. Following this revelation, much of the Alt-Right disavowed Mosley, and NPI stopped working with him. He assured his followers that he would be able to provide the paperwork that would back up his story. At the time of this writing, he has not done so.

Casey announced that he wanted to take Identity Evropa in a different direction, dropping any connection with the Alt-Right label, and referring to themselves strictly as "Identitarians." He also declared that they would no longer take part in large-scale demonstrations that were announced publicly beforehand, instead focusing entirely on smaller events limited to the group's members.[6]

### What Was the "Unite the Right" Rally?

Although it was not the first Alt-Right protest, the "Unite the Right" rally was the most notorious real-world Alt-Right event to date, making headlines across the globe. The purported catalyst for the event was the decision by the city of Charlottesville, Virginia, to remove a statue of Robert E. Lee from Emancipation Park. This decision was part of a larger trend throughout the South. Following Dylann Roof's racist shooting rampage in 2015, there was new pressure to remove Confederate monuments from public spaces.

Aside from the immediate cause of Confederate statues, "Unite the Right" was meant to be a pivotal moment for the Alt-Right, signifying that it was moving off the Internet and into public spaces in the real world. It was intended to show that it was now a real political movement, with real public supporters, and had moved beyond being a group of online trolls and propagandists.

Jason Kessler, an Alt-Right activist and Charlottesville resident, organized the protest, which was scheduled for August 11–12, 2017. Kessler and others worked with the city of Charlottesville to secure permits for the event. Although "Unite the Right" was the most well known Alt-Right protest in Charlottesville, it was actually the third such protest that year. The first was an unannounced nighttime event led by Richard Spencer on May 13. Then, on July 8, a few dozen members of the Ku Klux Klan (KKK) held a protest of their own. Both events drew counterprotesters, but neither resulted in significant violence.

The organizers labeled the August rally "Unite the Right" because they hoped to show the unity and size of the far right. It brought together many disparate elements of the radical right, including white nationalist groups that operated more like White Nationalism 1.0 (see chapter 2) organizations than Alt-Right groups. Members of the KKK also attended, and the rally drew the groups associated with the new umbrella organization, the Nationalist Front—the TWP, The League of the South, and the NSM. Some militia groups were present, though they insisted that they came to support the First Amendment rights of the protesters rather than to endorse the rally's message.

Many people who came to "Unite the Right" were not affiliated with any formal organizations. Some were part of informal meetup groups associated with Alt-Right websites, such as *The Daily Stormer* or *The Right Stuff*. Many of the most significant names in the Alt-Right attended the event, including Spencer, Mike Enoch, Matt Heimbach, Baked Alaska, Daniel Friberg, and James Allsup. David Duke also attended. The event's organizers sought to maintain certain aesthetic standards for the rally. Instead of the outrageous costumes associated with the KKK or neo-Nazism, attendees were encouraged to wear polo shirts and khakis.

On August 11, the night before the main rally, the Alt-Right attendees already in Charlottesville held a torchlight march through the University of Virginia. Throughout the march, they shouted slogans that are now associated with the Alt-Right, including the catchphrase, "Jews will not replace us." That night, the Alt-Right significantly outnumbered the counterprotesters, and there were minor scuffles between the two groups. The Alt-Right viewed the march as an overwhelming success. The following day's activities, however, did not go according to the organizers' plans.

On August 12, counterprotesters greatly outnumbered Alt-Right protesters. These counterprotesters included many representatives from the far left, including communist, anarchist, and Antifa groups. Other more mainstream groups and individuals also joined the counterprotest, including representatives from the National Council of Churches, as well as ordinary Charlottesville residents. Many people in the Alt-Right arrived prepared for violence, carrying shields and wearing various kinds of armor.

The "Unite the Right" rally differed from most other large white nationalist demonstrations in a critical respect. It appears that local authorities made comparatively little effort to keep protesters separated from counterprotesters. These kinds of white nationalist events typically follow a pattern, especially when the ralliers announce their plans to the local government and request permits: The far-right protesters follow a designated path to the place where they have permission to rally;

counterprotesters have their own designated space. The two sides hurl epithets at each other from across barricades, but police are nearby to keep the two sides mostly separated.

On August 12, clashes between the two sides broke out well before the official speeches were scheduled to begin. Counterprotesters attacked the Alt-Right attendees with pepper spray and threw bricks and bottles. Both sides attacked each other with clubs. One Alt-Right protester, a member of the KKK, was filmed firing his rifle at the ground in the counterprotesters' direction. He was later arrested. Many people were seriously injured in the melee, some requiring hospitalization.

Because of these clashes, the governor of Virginia declared a state of emergency. Shortly afterward, before the rally was scheduled to officially begin, Virginia police declared that the event was an unlawful assembly, and riot police cleared the Alt-Right attendees from the park. This created a new wave of violence, as leaving the park required the rally goers to once again walk through throngs of counterprotesters.

The rally turned deadly two hours after the police initially dispersed the protesters. A young man named James Fields allegedly drove his car into a crowd of antiracist protesters, killing one—a counterprotester named Heather Heyer— and injuring nineteen others. The incident was captured on video. Fields was subsequently arrested and charged with second-degree murder, malicious wounding, and failure to stop following an accident. Several months later, prosecutors upgraded the charge to first-degree murder.[7] At the time of this writing, Fields's trial has not begun.

Prior to "Unite the Right," Fields was not a known figure in the Alt-Right. Photos taken earlier in the day showed him carrying a shield with the logo of a small white nationalist organization called Vanguard America, though the group denies that he was a member.

The facts of the case will be better understood following Fields's trial. In the incident's immediate aftermath, however, the two sides provided conflicting narratives of the event. The counterprotesters described it as a deliberate act of terrorism. People in the Alt-Right described it as an accident that occurred when Fields panicked after he found himself isolated and surrounded by threatening counterprotesters.

There were two additional deaths near the "Unite the Right" rally that day. Later that afternoon, a police helicopter crashed outside of Charlottesville, killing two Virginia state troopers. At the time of this writing, the cause of the crash is still under investigation, but no evidence has been released indicating that anyone involved with "Unite the Right" was responsible. Nonetheless, commentary about the rally often states that it led to the deaths of three people (Heyer and the state troopers).

"Unite the Right" was the largest white nationalist gathering in over a decade. Before authorities dispersed the rally, hundreds of attendees were present. The final tally may have been even higher had the rally continued; multiple people reported that they were on the way to the event before it was abruptly cancelled.

### What Were the Consequences of the "Unite the Right" Rally?

Following "Unite the Right," the Alt-Right made headlines across the globe like never before. It dominated the news for days. "Unite the Right" was uniformly denounced by prominent Republicans and Democrats. Speaker of the House Paul Ryan, House minority leader Nancy Pelosi, and Virginia governor Terry McAuliffe all expressed their outrage, as did former presidents Barack Obama and Bill Clinton. Attorney General Jeff Sessions denounced the event and the "domestic terrorism" that took place. Foreign leaders such as German chancellor Angela Merkel expressed their disgust with the images from Charlottesville. Even Steve Bannon took a swipe at the Alt-Right, saying, "Ethno-nationalism—it's losers. It's a fringe element. I think the media plays it up too much, and we gotta help crush it, you know, uh, help crush it more."[8]

President Donald Trump created a new controversy when he failed to denounce the rally unequivocally. Whereas most major political figures declared that the white nationalists were entirely to blame for the violence, Trump said that both sides shared responsibility. Days after the event, Trump declared, "You had a group on one side that was bad, and you had a group on the other side that was also very violent, and nobody wants to say that, but I'll say it right now."[9] Trump suggested that the extreme right and the extreme left were just mirror images of each other when he added, "What about the 'alt-left' that came charging at, as you say, the 'alt-right,' do they have any semblance of guilt? What about the fact they came charging with clubs in hands, swinging clubs, do they have any problem? I think they do."

President Trump's refusal to assign the Alt-Right all the blame for the violence in Charlottesville was part of a larger pattern. Throughout the 2016 presidential campaign, Trump refused to attack his Alt-Right supporters and did not explicitly distance himself from the Alt-Right until after the election was over (see the section "How Has President Trump Responded to His Support from the Alt-Right?" in chapter 8). The Alt-Right was delighted by Trump's response to "Unite the Right," though his words caused him problems with other allies. Important chief executive officers (CEOs) resigned from Trump's American Manufacturing Council, leading to the group's dissolution. Other former allies also attacked Trump. Julius Krein, who had previously supported Trump and founded the journal *American Affairs*, which seeks to provide an intellectual framework for Trumpism, announced that he regretted voting for him. According to Krein, "Either Mr. Trump is genuinely sympathetic to the David Duke types, or he is so obtuse as to be utterly incapable of learning from his worst mistakes. Either way, he continues to prove his harshest critics right."[10]

Many critics also lambasted the city of Charlottesville for its mishandling of the event. The nonprofit organization

ProPublica chastised the local police, noting that they "did little to stop the bloodshed."[11] The police department defended its actions, stating that the problems resulted from "Unite the Right" attendees' failure to enter the park from the agreed-upon direction.[12]

Prior to "Unite the Right," it was largely true that all publicity, even negative publicity, benefited the Alt-Right. Although media coverage of the Alt-Right is almost uniformly negative, it draws attention to the movement and raises its profile. After "Unite the Right," there was an acrimonious debate within the Alt-Right about whether the rally was successful from a propaganda perspective. Some insisted that it was, whereas others described it as a total disaster. Looking back on it several months later, it is clear that "Unite the Right" caused the Alt-Right significant harm.

Following the rally, in which Alt-Right supporters marched openly, making no effort to hide their faces, the movement experienced a new round of doxings. Whereas earlier doxings targeted major leaders and content creators, this time ordinary people who attended the rally faced major repercussions. For example, one attendee whose identity was uncovered subsequently lost his job at a hot dog restaurant. A number of undergraduate students were also identified, leading their universities to make statements condemning racism. If "Unite the Right" was intended to demonstrate that the Alt-Right had become a normal part of American politics, and that people in the movement could now be more open in their views, it failed miserably.

"Unite the Right" set off a new wave of no-platforming (see the section "What Is No-Platforming?" in chapter 10), creating new challenges for the movement on the Internet and hamstringing its ability to raise money. Although the organizers hoped that the rally would create new unity within the movement, the subsequent infighting created new fractures. For weeks, people in the Alt-Right engaged in vitriolic debates about optics and how the movement should organize in the future. Many people disengaged with the Alt-Right entirely.

Although this is difficult to measure quantitatively, it also seems that "Unite the Right" changed the public's perception of the Alt-Right. The Alt-Right had previously sought to distance itself from its precursors of White Nationalism 1.0 (see chapter 2). Although its main figures openly called for the creation of a racially pure white ethnostate, they tried to create a brand that was qualitatively different from the KKK, the National Alliance, and Aryan Nations. Before "Unite the Right," some observers still viewed the Alt-Right as an online band of irreverent, right-wing court jesters. Afterward, this perception was permanently lost.

## What Is the Alt-Right Corporation?

The Alt-Right Corporation sought to unite some of the most significant figures and groups in the Alt-Right into a single organization. Its primary vehicle was a new website, *Altright. com*. At the start, its leadership contained some of the most important names in the Alt-Right movement in the United States and Europe. The website's initial editors included Richard Spencer of the NPI, Daniel Friberg of Arktos Publishing, Henrik Palmgren of Red Ice Radio, Hunter Wallace of the Southern nationalist website *Occidental Dissent*, and a relative newcomer to the Alt-Right named Jason Jorjani, an academic of Persian ancestry with a particular interest in Iranian politics. William Regnery, the white nationalist philanthropist, was listed as the publisher.

The website was similar to Spencer's previous online platforms, such as *Alternative Right* and *Radix Journal*. It posted regular articles and podcasts, but it also included many videos. The site also promised that it would eventually host an online forum. At its inception, the Alt-Right Corporation looked like it would be the most significant organization in the movement.

However, the organization experienced several setbacks during its first year. The site's forum was only briefly active before the platform that hosted it, Discord, shut it down. Many of the people involved with the group have subsequently left. Wallace's name came off the masthead after just a few months, and he stopped posting content on the site. Red Ice Radio and the Alt-Right Corporation also apparently cut ties with each other in late 2017. In both cases, the parties involved did not provide any public explanation for the split.

Jason Jorjani's departure from the organization was more dramatic. Jorjani was always ideologically distinct from the rest of the Alt-Right. Although he previously worked for Arktos Publishing, which publishes far-right books, white nationalism has never been Jorjani's primary interest. His work has instead focused on philosophy and Zoroastrianism. He is involved with the Iranian Renaissance movement, which seeks the end of the Islamic government in that country. Shortly after the "Unite the Right" rally, Jorjani resigned from both the Alt-Right Corporation and Arktos, stating his desire to focus on Iranian politics. He had previously promised his colleagues that he would be able to secure a massive amount of funding for the Alt-Right from unknown foreign sources, but this apparently never materialized. Both Spencer and Jorjani published hostile accounts of their experiences with each other after the split.

The Alt-Right Corporation remains a significant element of the larger Alt-Right, but it has not at this point united the movement.

### Are There Alt-Right Politicians?

At the time of this writing, there are no significant elected officials or notable candidates in the United States who identify with the Alt-Right. White nationalists have obviously sought public office in the past. George Lincoln Rockwell ran for governor of Virginia. David Duke briefly served in the Louisiana legislature and unsuccessfully sought statewide office and the presidency. Since the birth of the Alt-Right as a concept, open supporters of the movement have generally avoided electoral politics.

Augustus Sol Invictus made an unsuccessful bid to be the Libertarian Party's nominee for the 2016 U.S. Senate election in Florida. He was later scheduled to speak at the "Unite the Right" rally in Charlottesville, Virginia. The TWP also endorsed a small number of unsuccessful candidates. Richard Spencer floated the idea of running for Montana's sole congressional seat, but he apparently abandoned the idea. A white nationalist and extreme anti-Semite named Patrick Little ran in the 2018 California U.S. Senate primary election, and earned a little more than 1 percent of the vote.

Paul Nehlen of Wisconsin is, at present, the most notable Alt-Right candidate for political office. In 2016, Nehlen challenged Paul Ryan in the Republican primaries. Ryan won in a landslide, but Nehlen promised to seek that office again in 2018. Nehlen has retweeted Alt-Right accounts on a number of occasions and often uses terms that originated from the Alt-Right. For example, Nehlen has appeared on the well-known Alt-Right podcast *Fash the Nation*. During that appearance, he demonstrated his familiarity with Alt-Right lingo, describing himself as "red-pilled on globalism, RR and JQ."[13] "RR" stands for "race realism," and "JQ" stands for the Jewish Question—a reference to the anti-Semitic theory that Jews have undue influence on American life and use that influence to harm white people.

Until recently, Nehlen was not a fringe figure in conservative politics, despite his poor showing in his most recent political campaign. He spoke at a rally in favor of Roy Moore during the 2017 Alabama special election for U.S. Senate— Moore, who was accused of sexual misconduct, narrowly lost that election. Nehlen has also appeared with Steve Bannon.

Nehlen's increasingly outspoken far-right views eventually cost him support from more mainstream figures. Following his appearance on *Fash the Nation* and a series of tweets in which Nehlen endorsed Kevin MacDonald's book on Jewish influence, Steve Bannon cut all ties with him. One of Bannon's advisors subsequently remarked, "Nehlen is dead to us."[14] Nehlen was also subsequently banned from Twitter. He continued to post on Gab, a social media site that has fewer speech restrictions, until he was kicked off of that site, as well. He was banned from Gab for revealing the personal information of a fellow Alt-Right supporter who used the name Ricky Vaughn. As a result of this, much of the Alt-Right turned on Nehlen.

Corey Stewart, who repeated some Alt-Right slogans and talking points, sought the GOP's gubernatorial nomination in Virginia in 2016. Stewart made defending Confederate symbols a key part of his campaign. He also adopted the Alt-Right slur *cuckservative*[15] when discussing his opponent, Ed Gillespie—though shortly before the primary election, he did "condemn the Klan and all those racist groups."[16] Stewart lost the Republican primary to Gillespie, who subsequently lost to the Democrat Ralph Northam. Stewart again sought public office in 2018, winning the Republican nomination for U.S. Senate. At the time of this writing, it is unknown how he will perform in the general election.

For now, most open and prominent Alt-Right supporters remain aloof from the electoral process. They show enthusiasm for Republican candidates that repeat their talking points, but at the time of this writing, there is little danger that the Alt-Right will become a white nationalist equivalent of the Tea Party, regularly unseating Republicans who do not endorse white nationalism. Neither is there significant danger that an Alt-Right third party will enjoy meaningful success in the political process in the near future. Such parties do occasionally spring up; the American Freedom Party (formerly the American Third Position Party) has made it onto the ballot in a number of races—including several states in the 2012 presidential election—but it has never earned more than 1 percent of the vote in any election.

## What Is the "Mainstream Versus Vanguard" Debate?

There are many debates within the Alt-Right. Many of these discussions are around ideological questions and the movement's long-term goals. The most acrimonious disputes often center on questions of strategy and tactics. Specifically, people within the Alt-Right do not agree on how they should present themselves and their message. This battle precedes the formation of the Alt-Right by many decades; white nationalists have always argued about these questions. For a thorough discussion of these debates, I recommend Leonard Zeskind's book, *Blood and Politics*.

These arguments commonly revolve around whether the movement should present itself as mainstream, approachable, and moderate, or if it should represent a radical vanguard, brazenly expressing its extreme opinions in an outrageous manner. Those pushing a mainstream approach say that white nationalists should recognize that they are a hated minority; most white Americans, even those with a high level of racial anxiety, oppose them. They thus have little chance to influence politics directly. For that reason, according to this view, white nationalists need to downplay their radicalism; they should engage in normal partisan politics, only using subtle dog-whistle racism in their campaigns, and deny that they are motivated by racism. The mainstream approach would also entail joining ordinary political parties and pushing for policies that white nationalists support.

In contrast, those who take the vanguard approach say that white nationalists need to promote their agenda aggressively at every opportunity. They argue that they need to be open about their views, as this is the only way that they can eventually be normalized. This variety of white nationalist argues that radicalism is necessary because they do not have time to work quietly behind the scenes, promoting marginal changes that benefit whites.

# THE ALT-RIGHT AND CONSERVATISM

### *What Does It Mean to Be Right Wing?*

The Alt-Right is a right-wing movement, as is mainstream conservatism. Yet the two ideological camps do not overlap very much when it comes to foundational principles. The term *right wing* encompasses a large number of divergent ideological tendencies, including radical libertarians, explicit fascists, and Burkean conservatives. The left is similarly diverse, including everything from left-wing anarchists, moderate "New Democrats" like former president Bill Clinton, and totalitarian communists. Given these expansive categories, one may question whether the concepts of left and right have any real utility.

Many groups and individuals have offered different definitions of these terms. Some argue that the political spectrum refers to where one stands on the question of individual liberty, with complete freedom representing the far right and authoritarianism representing the far left. Such a categorization seems to preclude the possibility of right-wing authoritarianism. Indeed, a number of conservatives and libertarians attempt to categorize Nazism as a left-wing movement—arguing that National Socialism was left-wing because it rejected individual liberty. Conservative author Dinesh D'Souza made this argument recently in his 2017 book *The Big Lie: Exposing the Nazi Roots of the American Left*. Those who prefer this taxonomy have unsurprisingly attempted to label the Alt-Right as a left-wing movement.[1]

Although this description of the left-right ideological divide is popular among many conservatives and libertarians, it is has little support among academic political theorists. The Italian scholar Norberto Bobbio provided one of the more useful definitions of *left* and *right*, which is sufficiently broad to capture most ideological groups and yet still provides a meaningful distinction between left and right. According to Bobbio, left and right are ultimately defined by their respective views on equality and hierarchy, with the left emphasizing the former and the right mostly emphasizing the latter.[2] By this definition, the Alt-Right, which entirely rejects equality as a goal, is obviously a right-wing movement. It is also far to the right of American conservatives, who do not rank equality as the most important political goal but nonetheless do not usually reject it as an ideal.

### What Is Conservatism?

When the Alt-Right first appeared, the movement defined itself almost exclusively in negative terms. That is, *Alt-Right* could encompass almost anyone right-of-center who rejected the mainstream conservative movement. In this sense, it could apply just as well to white nationalists, paleoconservatives, and libertarians. To understand what they were reacting against, however, we must understand the conservative movement.

*Conservatism* is difficult to define. The hazy nature of conservatism, in the broadest definition of the term, is one reason that it has such staying power. If we define conservatism simply as a fear of radical change, then all societies always have a large proportion of conservatives.

Although conservatism as a general disposition has always existed, the American conservative movement that we know today was born in the postwar years. A couple of dates are reasonable candidates for marking the birth of modern conservatism. The 1953 publication of Russell Kirk's best-known work, *The Conservative Mind*, was one such moment. This book made Kirk a significant public intellectual, and more important, made the case that conservatives had an impressive intellectual pedigree.

The inaugural issue of *National Review*, published in 1955, was perhaps even more significant. This journal of conservative opinion, which included many figures now considered the marquee names of conservatism, played an instrumental role in developing conservative political thought. The magazine was founded by a young journalist named William F. Buckley, Jr., who had already made a name for himself with his book *God and Man at Yale*, published in 1951, which argued that universities had abandoned their traditional mission in favor of anticapitalist and anti-Christian indoctrination.

In subsequent years, conservatism came to define itself as a defense of three principles: free-market capitalism, traditional values, and anticommunism (which was later expanded to encompass strong national defense more broadly). On their face, these principles are connected only loosely; there does not seem to be an obvious connection between tax cuts and a defense of traditional cultural norms, for example. However, conservative theorists insisted that these various values all depended on each other. Frank Meyer, also associated with *National Review*, played an important role in developing a coherent conservative political philosophy.

According to Meyer, who made his case in the pages of *National Review* and in his book *In Defense of Freedom*, liberty and traditional morality depended upon each other. He argued that people must make virtuous decisions without coercion. If people are not free, they are not exercising genuine virtue. Similarly, a free society requires a virtuous people. In the absence of widespread private virtue, a strong state will be necessary to maintain order. Anticommunism, of course, was vital to the other two principles, as a powerful, expansionist, atheist, and anticapitalist Soviet Union represented an existential threat to conservative values.

Conservatism continued to evolve, and major conservative figures have taken different views on policy issues, but the basic principles that most conservatives embrace have remained the same since the 1960s.

### Is Conservatism a Universalist Ideology?

For many decades, mainstream American conservatives have argued that their philosophical principles are universal, equally applicable to all demographic groups domestically and across the globe. This sets American conservatives apart from other varieties of conservatism that developed elsewhere— other kinds of conservatism are explicit defenses of a particular people's unique cultural folkways and institutions. According to most American conservatives, the causes of economic freedom and traditional cultural norms are beneficial to all and could be politically appealing to all; they therefore claim to reject explicit identity politics. As one prominent conservative journalist put it, "Conservatives hoist their ideas on flagpoles and see who salutes."[3]

Conservatives are eager to demonstrate their movement's racial, gender, and religious diversity. Their ranks include a number of influential African American intellectuals such as Thomas Sowell and Shelby Steele, politicians such as Republican senator Tim Scott of South Carolina, and Supreme Court justice Clarence Thomas. Conservatives market many of their preferred policies—such as school choice and enterprise zones—as being designed specifically to uplift underprivileged minorities.

Conservative foreign policy during President George W. Bush's time in office was based on the notion that democracy is the ideal system for all societies and that the expansion of political liberty around the globe is indispensable to American security. As Bush put it in his second inaugural

address: "We have confidence because freedom is the permanent hope of mankind, the hunger in dark places, the longing
of the soul."[4]

Mainstream conservatives are not unified on the question
of immigration, though on average, they are less progressive on this question than liberals. But today's conservatives
are mostly consistent in their claim that support for immigration restrictions are not the result of ethnic or racial animosity, preferring instead to speak about legality, economic
consequences, and assimilation. A number of important
conservative voices are pro-immigration. There are many
conservative arguments that one can make in favor of generous immigration policies. Although this is an empirical
question that people disagree on, many conservative and libertarian economists argue that immigration is good for the
national economy and should be supported for that reason.
Other conservatives have noted that immigration has been
crucial to economic and political development throughout
American history, and thus radical new restrictions would
represent a break with American tradition and perhaps even
be un-American.

Although conservatism's premises are not explicitly exclusionary and people of all races, ethnicities, and religions
describe themselves as conservatives, self-described
conservatives are not evenly distributed across all major demographic groups. To this day, white men remain the most likely
group to describe themselves as conservatives.

Progressives often push back against conservatives who
claim that they reject racism and white identity politics.
They note accurately that most conservative intellectuals and
journalists were hostile to the Civil Rights Movement, and conservative politicians were happy to cater to racial anxieties to
attract votes from Southern whites. Most conservatives remain
hostile to policies such as affirmative action and are critical of
the Black Lives Matter movement and other social movements
that promote racial equity.

## How Did Conservatives Conquer the Republican Party?

By the early 1960s, the conservative movement had developed a coherent political platform, counted many important journalists and intellectuals within its ranks, and had a number of influential grass-roots organizations such as Young Americans for Freedom and the John Birch Society (JBS). In 1964, it demonstrated that it was the dominant force in the Republican Party when the archconservative Barry Goldwater defeated the more moderate Nelson Rockefeller in the GOP presidential primary. Goldwater subsequently lost the general election in a landslide. The defeat was a major setback for conservatism, but since the Goldwater nomination, conservative ideologues have been a dominant force in Republican politics.

Following Goldwater's defeat, conservatives continued to organize and developed a powerful fundraising apparatus. Although Goldwater lost, he enjoyed an impressive number of dedicated activists and had a large list of donors. A young conservative named Richard Viguerie suspected that these donors would be willing to give again. For this reason, after the election was over, he gathered the list of Goldwater donors and began to solicit contributions from them for other conservative causes. He ultimately became the father of conservative direct mail, which was a primary means of building the movement. Viguerie was soon employing hundreds of employees and raised massive sums for politicians like Jesse Helms and Strom Thurmond, and organizations such as the National Rifle Association and the National Right to Work Legal Foundation.[5]

Besides small donations that result from direct mail and other forms of solicitation, large-scale donors who eagerly spent their wealth on conservative causes proved indispensable to the movement. The public is well aware of the Koch brothers and the tremendous financial support that they provide to fiscally conservative and libertarian organizations. They are not unique, however. Other major philanthropists have lavished millions of dollars on conservative organizations.

The Heritage Foundation would probably not exist if not for the massive support from Joseph Coors, Sr.[6] Richard Scaife has given more than $200 million to various conservative and libertarian organizations.[7]

The conservative movement won relatively few significant victories during the 1970s. Although Richard Nixon worked to earn support from conservatives during his 1968 presidential campaign, he did not govern as a movement conservative, supporting many policies that outraged conservative journalists and intellectuals, such as price controls, the creation of the Environmental Protection Agency (EPA), and America's withdrawal from Vietnam. The Watergate scandal and Nixon's subsequent resignation helped set the stage for President Jimmy Carter's election and a new period of Democratic dominance.

Conservatives did not enjoy real power at the national level until the election of 1980, which sent Ronald Reagan to the White House. Conservatives were delighted to finally have a president who reliably advocated for the movement's principles—cutting taxes and regulations and increasing military spending. Although Reagan-era policies led to an explosion of the federal deficit, the 1980s also experienced a long period of economic growth and the end of the Cold War. Conservatives argued that Reagan vindicated both their fundamental principles and their policy proposals. Since that time, most GOP presidential contenders have felt it necessary to assure Republican voters that they are true and consistent conservatives in the Reagan mold.

Conservative groups and leaders continue to pressure Republican leaders to maintain consistent conservative policy stances. For example, Grover Norquist's organization, Americans for Tax Reform, encourages candidates and elected officials to sign a "taxpayer protection pledge," in which they agree always to vote against tax increases. The organization subsequently monitors these politicians to ensure that they follow through on this promise. Organizations like

FreedomWorks back primary challengers against incumbent Republicans whom they deem insufficiently conservative on economic issues.

Conservative voices in the media, especially talk radio, regularly criticize elected Republicans when they fail to maintain ideological purity. Moderate Republicans are often given the derisive title of *RINO* (which stands for "Republican In Name Only") and are warned that their failure to govern as conservatives will cost them support from their base.

### What Is Neoconservatism?

The first neoconservatives were refugees from the political left who entered the conservative movement in the 1960s and 1970s. These new conservatives tended to differ from the older generation of conservatives, as well as from the base of the Republican Party. The first generation of neoconservatives was predominantly, though not exclusively, Jewish and lived in major East Coast cities such as New York and Washington, D.C. Some of these figures had once been ideologically aligned with the far left—admiration for Leon Trotsky, for example, was a common trait.

Every individual had different justifications, but there were a few common reasons that neoconservatives tended to move to the right. Some neoconservatives argued that American liberals had moved too far to the left over the course of the 1960s. As left-wing groups such as Students for a Democratic Society, the Black Panthers, Maoist groups, and similar organizations became the face of the left, they made many moderate liberals uneasy. Others were unnerved by the left's new and growing opposition to Israel, especially after the 1967 Six-Day War, which caused some people to conclude that the American left was taking an anti-Semitic turn.

In terms of actual policy, when the Great Society and other major liberal policy initiatives failed to achieve their promised objectives, some of these policies' former supporters began to rethink their earlier positions. As Irving Kristol, the father of neoconservatism, put it: "[A] neoconservative is a liberal who was mugged by reality."[8] Not all people described as neoconservatives became Republicans. Democratic senators such as Daniel Patrick Moynihan and Henry "Scoop" Jackson have sometimes been called neoconservative.

Although they were an ideologically heterogeneous group, the neoconservatives tended to differ from other conservatives on a few important issues. They were generally more willing to accept the welfare state, for example. As Irving Kristol noted, people "need such assistance; they demand it; they will get it."[9] Neoconservatives also tended to be more hawkish than other conservatives. They were also, on average, more willing to support policies that promoted racial equality.

Most of the conservative movement was pleased when the neoconservatives joined their ranks, even if they had significant ideological differences. They provided the movement with a new intellectual energy and helped make conservatism more palatable to the nation's elites. Yet their arrival was also a source of tension, especially as they became increasingly powerful, eventually becoming the movement's most influential faction. Many people from the older conservative tradition, those who were eventually called *paleoconservatives* (see the section "What Is Paleoconservatism?" in chapter 4), resented the newcomers, noting that many of them had never really shed their earlier left-wing orientation, and in any event, they should defer to people whose involvement in the conservative movement long predated their own.

Disgust with neoconservatives was common among the first people who used the term *Alternative Right*, back when the term was mostly associated with *Taki's Magazine*. Although there are many reasons that one could criticize the neoconservatives, some critiques of the movement are transparently anti-Semitic. We can find people with beliefs consistent with neoconservatism from all racial, ethnic, and religious backgrounds, but it is true that the original neoconservatives were disproportionately Jewish. Right-wing conspiracy theorists have suggested that Jewish neoconservatives are more loyal to Israel than the United States, arguing that policies such as the Iraq War were really implemented to benefit Israel. Some anti-Semites, such as Kevin MacDonald, have fixated on neoconservatism's Jewish nature, arguing that Jews have used their perch in the conservative movement to advance their own interests at the expense of non-Jewish white Americans.

### How Have Conservatives Dealt with Racial Issues?

Self-described conservatives are heterogeneous when it comes to racial attitudes, although public opinion polling consistently shows that conservatives are, on average and controlling for all other variables, less progressive on racial questions than liberals are. The mainstream conservative movement's most important institutions, however, all claim that they oppose racism. Although maintaining white racial dominance has never been the stated primary concern of the conservative intellectual movement, it has often opposed new efforts to promote racial equality. *National Review*, for example, was officially opposed to major civil rights legislation during the 1950s and 1960s.[10] The magazine was similarly critical of Martin Luther King, Jr., during this period. Well into the 1980s, *National Review* continued to support apartheid in South Africa.

The Republican Party's leaders and the conservative movement more broadly were eager to take advantage of the split among the Democrats over racial issues. As the progressive elements of the Democratic Party insisted on civil rights being a critical element of the party platform, it caused a rift with the Southern wing of the party. The South had been solidly Democratic since Reconstruction, and Southern support was one reason why the Democrats were so powerful during the New Deal era and beyond. These Southern Democrats, however, remained racial conservatives, opposing civil rights legislation and executive actions to foster equality.

Eventually, the Democratic Party was no longer able to hold these disparate elements together. The first major cracks appeared when Strom Thurmond, a Democrat from South Carolina, ran for president in 1948 as the candidate for the short-lived Dixiecrat Party. Thurmond won four Southern states. The GOP began to make its first significant inroads in the South in 1964. Although the Republican Barry Goldwater—who opposed civil rights legislation—lost that election in a landslide, he won five states in the Deep South. In 1968, the Democrats lost every Southern state but Texas— the rest supported either Nixon or the segregationist George Wallace.

Republicans realized that they had an opportunity to redraw the electoral map by appealing to white anxiety in the wake of new progressive racial policies promoted by the Democrats. The so-called Southern Strategy eventually made the South one of the most consistently Republican regions of the country. As Nixon strategist Kevin P. Phillips put it in 1969: "The principal force which broke the Democratic (New Deal) coalition is the Negro socioeconomic revolution and liberal Democratic ideological inability to cope with it."[11]

Nonetheless, the mainstream conservative movement has evolved on questions of race. There is no doubt that the GOP has often appealed to racist dog whistles during electoral campaigns, and this has historically received little criticism from the conservative movement's leaders. However, conservatism tries to present itself as a color-blind and individualist political philosophy. When it attacks groups and individuals that lobby for racial causes, conservatives usually argue that they are against identity politics as such. That is, they oppose all forms of racial or ethnic collectivism and solidarity, regardless of the group and its constituents.

## What Has Been Conservatism's Response to Open Racism in Its Ranks?

Just as conservatism has evolved on questions of race, so has it changed its attitudes toward explicit racists that describe themselves as conservative. Since the movement's inception, conservatives have set explicit boundaries of acceptable opinion and expelled people who crossed those boundaries. As American society has changed in recent decades, moving in a more egalitarian direction, conservatives have similarly changed what constitutes an unacceptable opinion. The movement has thus engaged in periodic housecleaning, purging from its ranks those groups and individuals they deemed dangerous to both the movement and overall social harmony. Open racism or anti-Semitism was often a key reason why a group or individual has been expelled from conservative circles. William F. Buckley was a critical figure in this regard, though he was not a consistent antiracist.

Buckley's influence was first displayed when he took on the JBS in the 1960s. At the time, the society was the largest grassroots conservative organization in the United States. Buckley's problem with the JBS was not that it was racist or anti-Semitic, but that its leader, Robert Welch, was a paranoid conspiracy theorist, convinced that the Kremlin secretly controlled the highest levels of the U.S. government. Welch was a stumbling block to conservatism's goal of establishing itself as a respectable ideology and political movement. Following Buckley's attacks on the JBS, the organization went into a steep decline, and within a few years, it was tiny and inconsequential, although it still exists today.

In subsequent decades, Buckley played an important role in distancing conservatism from outspoken racists and anti-Semites. He forcefully denounced former Ku Klux Klan (KKK) leader David Duke during his many political campaigns, for example, and his intervention kept the paleoconservative Mel Bradford from receiving an important appointment in the Reagan administration (see the section "What Is Paleoconservatism?" in chapter 4). Bradford's admiration of the old Confederacy and antipathy toward Abraham Lincoln concerned several prominent conservatives, who demanded the position be given to William Bennett instead. This was a watershed moment, as it signaled that the GOP and conservatism more generally were ready to disassociate themselves from the paleoconservative voices that still embraced the movement's older racial conservatism.

In the early 1990s, Buckley attacked Patrick J. Buchanan and his own *National Review* colleague Joseph Sobran for their anti-Semitism. Sobran, once considered one of Buckley's most important protégés, was eventually removed from the magazine entirely due to his fixation on Israel and its supposedly negative influence on the United States. In subsequent decades, *National Review* has fired other contributors for crossing certain boundaries when it comes to race, such as John Derbyshire.

### Can the Conservative Movement Still Control Right-Wing Discourse in the United States?

Conservatism may be losing its ability to set meaningful boundaries in right-wing discourse, which may explain the rise of both Donald Trump and the Alt-Right. In the 1980s and 1990s, if mainstream conservatives shunned a person on the political right, he or she was left without a platform. *National Review* and a handful of other publications were the main sources of conservative opinion. AM talk radio show hosts and the Fox News Channel later joined them. Although progressives have many valid critiques of these venues, they did exercise a degree of editorial control over what they presented to the public. A person deemed unacceptable to any of these venues was reduced to cheap pamphleteering or sending out newsletters to mailing lists. This was the means by which open white nationalists spread their propaganda throughout most of that movement's history, and it was not very effective.

Although still powerful, more traditional sources of news are at a nadir of influence. Print publications of all ideological inclinations are experiencing declining circulations. *Human Events*, once the most important conservative newspaper, no longer even runs a print edition. The audience for programs like Rush Limbaugh's radio show is massive, but these listeners tend to be old—in their sixties or older. As of 2014, the median age of Fox News Channel viewers was 68.[12] Young Americans increasingly get their news from online sources.

Creating a new cable television station is astronomically expensive. This is also true of print publications. In fact, throughout its history, *National Review* has never turned a profit; it relies heavily on donations to stay afloat. The Internet is a different media landscape. It is possible to create a website for free, and a quality website can be created and maintained for a few hundred dollars a year or less. This creates new opportunities for voices that are shut out of the mainstream discussion.

People across the ideological landscape are taking advantage of the Internet to build unprecedented audiences for their ideas. Adherents to the Alt-Right are among them, and together they have built a media apparatus that is completely separate from the mainstream conservative movement. The Alt-Right, for the most part, has no interest in infiltrating conservative media institutions, as it has platforms of its own. Unlike the major conservative platforms, most Alt-Right websites do not have the funds to pay people for content, or they can pay only a trifling sum. In this sense, it remains disadvantaged compared to the conservative movement, which has the resources to support a large number of full-time polemicists. However, the Alt-Right has no shortage of volunteer propagandists willing to put considerable time into constructing their messages and spreading them online.

Mainstream conservatism also suffers from a credibility problem, as Donald Trump's presidential campaign demonstrated. There was a time when the main spokespeople of the conservative movement exercised considerable influence over the Republican Party and partisan politics. There were many cases when Buckley's personal intervention played an enormous role in keeping the American right within certain boundaries. The conservative movement no longer has any figures with that kind of stature. When *National Review* published an entire issue focused on attacking Trump during the 2016 GOP primaries, it had no apparent effect. Nor did it apparently matter when leading conservatives, such as columnist George F. Will, denounced Trump (and continue to do so now that he is president).

Despite these challenges, however, it would be a mistake to discount the conservative movement's continued influence on the GOP. Although they were not able to keep Donald Trump from securing the Republican nomination, after he entered the White House, he mostly filled his cabinet with conventional conservatives. President Trump's policy agenda has been generically conservative, for the most part. Mainstream conservative websites continue to enjoy far more traffic than even the most popular Alt-Right platforms.

### What Does the Alt-Right Think of the Conservative Movement?

The Alt-Right hates the conservative movement, perhaps considering it a greater hindrance to their goals than the left. They attack it for its focus on economic questions and hesitancy to engage directly with the issue of race. According to the Alt-Right, conservatives obsess over tax cuts, deregulation, and other small bourgeois concerns, but they fear tackling demographic questions, which the Alt-Right consider existential. The Alt-Right argues that conservatives focus on economic questions out of cowardice rather than principle. That is, its proponents say that conservatives are terrified of being accused of racism, and to avoid the charge, they tiptoe around racial questions, ceding the subject to the left.

Because the Alt-Right does not possess a single, unifying ideology other than white identity politics, the movement contains diverse opinions when it comes to public policies. However, we can speak broadly about the kinds of policies that the Alt-Right supports and opposes. This is especially true of questions pertaining to race and immigration. Although conservatives tend to be more restrictionist on immigration than progressives, the Alt-Right is much more radical, as it wants to end all nonwhite immigration.

Conservatives typically call for the government to be color-blind, whereas the Alt-Right wants the government to openly favor white people. Like many on the left, white nationalists accuse conservatives (especially Republican politicians) of quietly stoking white racial anxiety to win elections. However, the Alt-Right contends that conservatives never follow through to implement policies specifically designed to advance white interests. They note that Republicans have never taken direct action to slow or halt America's transition to a majority nonwhite country.

### What Is the Alt-Right's Stance on the Religious Right?

Although there are Alt-Right Christians, the general movement opposes most institutions associated with mainstream Christianity in the United States, including conservative Christianity. The Alt-Right has many complaints with these institutions. According to the Alt-Right, it is a problem that most Christian denominations officially and explicitly oppose racism. Although the Christian right in the United States once organized in opposition to forced racial segregation in schools, no significant denomination or mainstream Christian group maintains this position today. Since the Alt-Right began receiving significant media attention, many major Christian denominations and other Christian organizations have issued formal statements denouncing the movement and reaffirming their commitment to racial equality.

Prominent white nationalists like William Pierce, Revilo P. Oliver, and Ben Klassen viewed Christianity as a major stumbling block to overcome. White nationalists make a number of common complaints about Christianity. As a universal religion, open to all people, Christianity weakens ethnocentrism; Christians are presumably supposed to place their religion before their race, and many white nationalists argue that race should be white people's dominant concern. Jews play a central role in the Christian Bible, and according to white nationalists, this makes it easier for Jewish people to manipulate white Gentiles into favoring policies that are against their interests. Christianity did not originate in Europe, so it represents a foreign influence on white people. More broadly, white nationalists tend to echo Friedrich Nietzsche's critique of Christianity as a "slave morality" that values weakness over strength. For an introduction to white nationalism's relationship with Christianity, I recommend Damon Berry's book, *Blood and Faith: Christianity in American White Nationalism*.

Many of the Alt-Right's most prominent figures have similar feelings about Christianity. Richard Spencer and Greg Johnson, for example, have expressed their misgivings with Christianity. However, on average, the Alt-Right may be less opposed to Christianity than earlier white nationalist movements in the United States. Although acrimonious religious debates frequently break out on Alt-Right forums, the Alt-Right's leading voices avoid talking about religion for the most part. They criticize Christian leaders that push for higher immigration rates and multiculturalism, but the Alt-Right is less likely to denounce Christianity as such.

Overall, however, the Alt-Right views the religious right as a negative phenomenon because its energies are not devoted to white racial preservation. Beyond this, much of the Alt-Right disagrees with the religious right on questions of public policy. Abortion remains the most important policy issue to the religious right. Although the Alt-Right is not in total agreement on this question, much of that movement is pro-choice. They do not favor access to abortion because they care about women's autonomy, however. Instead, the pro-choice element of the Alt-Right believes that abortion is helpful because it keeps the minority population from growing at a faster rate, and it is purportedly eugenic in a broader sense as well.

## How Does the Alt-Right Differ from Conservatism on Foreign Policy?

The Alt-Right rejects the mainstream conservative view on foreign affairs. When it comes to specific policies, the Alt-Right's positions are often similar to those of the left, though they are grounded in a different worldview. The Alt-Right overall opposes America's close relationship with Israel. Unlike Israel's critics on other points of the political spectrum, anti-Semitism, rather than concern about Israeli mistreatment of Palestinians, drives the Alt-Right's feelings about this issue.

The Alt-Right also opposes neoconservative foreign policies, such as military intervention in the Middle East. They have offered a few different explanations for this position. Some argue that American interventions are the result of Israel's influence on U.S. foreign policy, and that support for Israel is the real reason why the United States has such a conspicuous presence in the Middle East. Others in the Alt-Right have opposed these interventions because they disagree with the second President Bush's argument that democracy is the solution to international terrorism. They argue that these Middle Eastern countries are incapable of self-government, and authoritarians like Saddam Hussein and Muammar Gaddafi are the best possible leaders they can hope for. Concern that the destabilization of these countries will spur new waves of refugees into Europe or the United States is another common theme in Alt-Right material on foreign policy. These arguments are not mutually exclusive.

### What Are the Alt-Right's Views on Economics?

The Alt-Right does not have a unified stance on economic questions. Some people in the movement came from the libertarian tradition (see the section "What Is Libertarianism?" in chapter 4), and they still have mostly libertarian views on economic questions. Such people generally think that libertarianism can work, so long as the country is overwhelmingly white. Other voices in the Alt-Right are much more skeptical of capitalism and have been influenced by movements like the European New Right (ENR) (see the section "Who Is Alain de Benoist, and What Is the European New Right?" in chapter 3). This aspect of the Alt-Right argues that major corporations are largely to blame for America's turn toward the left on cultural issues. For example, they believe that the desire for cheap labor is a significant cause of mass immigration. They also note that the entertainment and advertising industries drive many of the cultural trends that they oppose, such as increasing acceptance of multiculturalism. Although there are few people in the Alt-Right who argue for outright socialism, many state that in a future ethnostate, big business will have less influence than it does today, and that the desire for higher profits must be reined in by a government focused on improving the race. The Traditionalist Worker Party (TWP) (see the section "Who Is Matthew Heimbach, and What Was the Traditionalist Worker Party?" in chapter 6) explicitly called for national socialism and argued that the Nazis had the ideal economic system.

### What Does the Alt-Right Mean by Cuckservative?

*Cuckservative* is a portmanteau of the words *conservative* and *cuckold*. The term is one of the most popular Alt-Right memes. Its general idea is that conservatives are working against their own future interests, whether they realize it or not. That is, according to the Alt-Right, conservatism requires a large white majority, as whites are the main supporters of conservative politics. However, the conservative movement refuses to support its own people, instead making persistent, ineffectual efforts to reach out to minority communities. The term is also meant to be emasculating.

### How Have Conservatives Responded to the Alt-Right?

When the Alt-Right began gaining significant media attention, some conservatives were quick to denounce the movement and insist that they rejected the Alt-Right's worldview entirely. As evidence for this, conservatives could point out (accurately) that they were frequent targets of Alt-Right vitriol. Conservatives obviously wanted to distance themselves from the Alt-Right, as any perceived connection between the two movements would undermine conservative efforts to shed their own reputation for racism and nativism.

Other conservatives argued that the Alt-Right was so insignificant that it did not deserve any media attention whatsoever. They suggested that the movement was being promoted by progressives as a way to discredit all conservatives—especially those who supported Trump.

Some conservatives, such as *National Review*'s David French, have regularly gone on the offensive against the Alt-Right, denouncing the movement for its racism and rejection of core American values. Such conservatives have subsequently faced a barrage of attacks from the Alt-Right, including harassment and death threats from anonymous trolls.

### Can the Alt-Right Copy the Conservative Model and Take Over the Republican Party?

Within living memory, we have seen an ideological movement effectively take control of a major political party, permanently shifting its philosophical foundation. The 1964 presidential primary represented the conservative conquest of the GOP (see the section "How Did Conservatives Conquer the Republican

Party?" earlier in this chapter). With organized conservatism in an apparently weakened state, one may wonder if a similar takeover is possible today. The fact that Donald Trump was able to capture the Republican nomination and the presidency in spite of conservative objections suggests that this could happen.

There are reasons to doubt this possibility, however. Well before one of their own (Reagan) earned the GOP presidential nomination, the conservative movement was a significant part of American public life. The JBS represented a massive grass-roots army, Young Americans for Freedom was successfully recruiting on college campuses across America, and magazines like *National Review* worked to develop a coherent conservative political theory and promote themselves as a significant intellectual force. Conservatives wrote bestselling books. Furthermore, although Republicans like Nelson Rockefeller were more moderate than the conservative movement preferred, the ideological chasm between moderate and conservative Republicans was not as great as that between the Alt-Right and today's mainstream conservatives.

Despite its current weaknesses, the conservative movement continues to control important institutions, and it remains the most powerful faction within the Republican Party. The Alt-Right may be effective at pushing its ideas on its own websites and on social media, and this is important, but it is dwarfed by conservative media, which includes talk radio, the Fox News Channel, and periodicals. Conservatives also have large student groups and grass-roots organizations. It is implausible to expect a group as small and underfunded as the Alt-Right to overthrow these organizations and assert itself as the new voice of the American right.

Furthermore, we should not overstate the importance to the Alt-Right of Trump's election. Whereas Goldwater was a true conservative in every meaningful sense, Trump cannot really be thought of as an Alt-Right president (see chapter 8), and I see little evidence that Alt-Right figures have subsequently taken any significant positions within the Trump administration (see the section "Are There Alt-Right Sympathizers in the Trump White House?" in chapter 8).

It may be the case, however, that the Alt-Right is having an indirect influence on the Republican Party and American politics that we cannot easily discern. Although conservatism was an unpopular view among intellectuals and media elites when *National Review* was created, it was not toxic in the way that white nationalism is today. Thus, people in the conservative movement may harbor these views privately, without expressing them. We cannot know how many people working in conservative institutions quietly hold Alt-Right viewpoints and consume Alt-Right material, but it is probably more than zero.

# 8

# THE ALT-RIGHT AND DONALD TRUMP

### Can Donald Trump Be Classified as Alt-Right?

We cannot accurately describe President Donald Trump as part of the Alt-Right. He is a right-wing populist, whose rhetoric has appealed to xenophobic elements of the electorate, but there is no compelling evidence that he is a white nationalist who seeks a pure white ethnostate. Saying that Trump is not part of the Alt-Right does not require endorsing his rhetoric or his administration's policies; it is simply a recognition of the Alt-Right's radicalism.

### Does Donald Trump Even Have a Consistent Ideology?

If we look through public statements that Donald Trump has made over his long career as a public figure, we quickly notice that he has not maintained consistent ideological positions. At times, he was to the left of the Republican Party, and at other times far to its right. Trump is not now, and has never been, a conservative in the sense that mainstream conservative intellectuals use the word.

Before he became a presidential candidate, Donald Trump took several positions that were at odds with many Republicans in the electorate. In some cases, he declared that his views had changed. Abortion was one issue that could have caused a problem for Trump, given the vocal minority of Republican voters who are passionate about the issue. He could not deny that he was once openly pro-choice. In 1999, Trump stated, "I am very pro-choice."[1] Trump claims that his attitude on abortion changed over the next decade. It appears that the first time Trump publicly declared that he was antiabortion occurred in 2011, when he gave a short speech at the Conservative Political Action Conference (CPAC). During that speech, Trump said little about abortion, but he did say, "I am pro-life."[2]

Trump also has been inconsistent on the issue of taxes, an issue that many conservatives consider sacrosanct. In the late 1990s, when he was considering a run for the presidency on the Reform Party ticket, Trump proposed a one-time, massive tax on America's super-rich as a way to reduce the national debt. Using language that would not sound out of place at an Occupy Wall Street rally, Trump declared, "By my calculations, 1 percent of Americans, who control 90 percent of the wealth in this country, would be affected by my plan."[3] Trump developed this idea in some detail in his 2000 book, *The America We Deserve.*[4] Had such a policy been implemented, it would have represented the largest single tax increase in American history. In that book, he also objected to certain tax policies being promoted by many conservatives, such as the flat tax, which would require all Americans to pay an identical tax rate. As president, however, he supported and signed a major tax cut, delighting mainstream conservatives.

There are issues where Trump has exhibited a great deal of consistency. The most obvious example is trade, where he typically echoes paleoconservative talking points (see the section "What Is Paleoconservatism?" in chapter 4). He has publicly accused other nations of "taking advantage of the United States" since the 1980s.[5] Trump lamented the U.S. trade deficit with other nations in 2000, noting that "we are being taken to the cleaners."[6] He has been generally consistent on this theme, although he did defend outsourcing on at least one occasion,[7] and many of his products have been manufactured abroad. He is especially critical of America's trade relationship with China, arguing that China has unfairly manipulated its currency to give itself an advantage. He even has referred to China as an "enemy," saying that it has "destroyed entire industries by utilizing low-wage workers, cost us tens of thousands of jobs, spied on our businesses, stolen our technology, and have manipulated and devalued their currency, which makes importing our goods more expensive—and sometimes, impossible."[8]

Although Trump has a long record of criticizing China, he has a consistent record of taking a conciliatory stance toward Russia—a stance that very much sets him apart from other leading Republicans but is congruent with the Alt-Right's views on the subject. He took such a position long before he entered Republican presidential primaries. In 2000, he argued that the United States needed to be firm when negotiating with Russia, but he also expressed sympathy for the country: "In a way, one has to feel sorry for Russia. It is like an old business or professional adversary who falls on hard times, loses his house, his wife, his money, starts drinking, and is found one day in the gutter. Natural human sympathy makes you want to get the guy on his feet, clean him up, give him a few bucks, and hope for the best."[9]

In 2015, when tensions with Russia were at a recent peak because of that country's annexation of Crimea and decision to back Bashar al-Assad in the Syrian civil war, most of the Republican presidential hopefuls took a markedly belligerent stance against Russian president Vladimir Putin. In contrast, Trump declared that he "would get along very well" with Putin. He also said, "He's running his country and at least he's a leader, unlike what we have in this country."[10] These generally positive feelings seem to be returned, as Putin described Trump as "bright and talented."[11] On the question of the Syrian civil war, Trump was the only leading Republican candidate who offered any rhetorical support for Russian intervention, stating, "Russia wants to get rid of ISIS. We want to get rid of

ISIS. Maybe let Russia do it. Let them get rid of ISIS. What the hell do we care?"[12]

Although Trump's generally positive stance toward Russia raised eyebrows among many mainstream commentators, his views on Iraq inspired rage from many conservatives. Although other Republicans have been critical of the George W. Bush administration's handling of the invasion and subsequent occupation of that country, Trump took this to a new level during a primary debate. He not only declared the entire project a mistake, he directly stated that the case for invasion had been built on lies: "They lied, they said there were weapons of mass destruction. There were none and they knew that there were none."[13] Beyond attacking the Iraq war, Trump challenged the argument that Bush had kept America safe from terrorism, noting that the September 11 attack occurred during Bush's presidency. As with his views on Russia, Trump's opinion on the Iraq War is similar to the Alt-Right's position.

Trump's overall stance when it comes to foreign policy, therefore, is somewhat confusing. He is not a principled non-interventionist like Ron or Rand Paul, but he is less of a committed internationalist than other Republican presidents. Trump did not position himself as the candidate of peace; he defended the use of torture and targeting the families of suspected terrorists.[14] Yet he has recited none of the usual neo-conservative talking points about spreading democracy to the Middle East.

During the 2016 campaign, many observers were troubled by Trump's use of the phrase "America first." For many, the term will always be associated with the America First Committee, an antiwar organization that thrived in the years before the Pearl Harbor attack that brought the United States into World War II. Although opposition to war is not necessarily problematic, the America First Committee also contained an element of anti-Semitism. This led the Anti-Defamation League (ADL) to encourage Trump to cease using the phrase. In a press release, ADL chief executive officer (CEO) Jonathan Greenblatt stated, "The undercurrents of anti-Semitism and bigotry that characterized the America First movement—including the assumption that Jews who opposed the movement had their own agenda and were not acting in America's best interest— is fortunately not a major concern today." Greenblatt went on, "However, for many Americans, the term 'America First' will always be associated with and tainted by this history. In a political season that already has prompted a national conversation about civility and tolerance, choosing a call to action historically associated with incivility and intolerance seems ill-advised."[15] The phrase "America first" was more recently employed by Patrick J. Buchanan, who called for a return to that policy in the 1990s. Buchanan has also faced accusations of anti-Semitism (see the section "What Is Paleoconservatism?" in chapter 4).

Trump has consistently taken a hard conservative stance on the issue of crime, as have many leading Republicans since the 1960s. Progressives often describe conservative talking points on crime as implicitly racist—as attempts to create fear among whites about minority criminals. Trump was a vocal supporter of Rudolph Giuliani's tough-on-crime policy when he was the mayor of New York City. Trump argued in 2000 that many affluent liberals are lenient on criminals because they can afford to insulate themselves from the costs of lawlessness: "I like to remind these friends that they would be singing a different tune if they didn't have a doorman downstairs, or if they had to walk through tough streets to get to work or the grocery store."[16] In 2015, he continued to take a hard-line position on crime, arguing that the nation's crime problem has gotten worse: "Violent crime in our cities is out of control. Murder rates are way up. There are far too many hardened drug dealers and gang members who are repeatedly involved in burglaries and drive-by killings. We need to get them off the streets so that they don't continue to terrorize their neighborhoods and ruin more lives."[17]

When it comes to his signature issue, immigration, Trump has shown a general consistency since 2000, with a few incongruities. Everyone is now well familiar with his negative statements about Mexicans from the speech that launched his campaign in 2015. But Trump had been a critic of current immigration policies for many years before that. He was openly hostile to undocumented immigrants and expressed his opposition to the current high levels of U.S. immigration in his 2000 book, *The America We Deserve*:

> Immigrant advocacy groups have no business rising up in protest, demanding special rights, services, and privileges. We can't allow ourselves to welcome outsiders out of kindness. If people enter this country by disregarding our laws, can we be confident that they will suddenly become law-abiding citizens once they arrive? A liberal policy of immigration may seem to reflect confidence and generosity. But our current laxness toward illegal immigration shows a recklessness and disregard for those who come here legally.[18]

Although his primary focus in that excerpt was illegal immigration, Trump also hinted that legal immigration may be too high when he said, "[L]et's be extremely careful not to admit more people than we can absorb. It comes down to this: We must take care of our own people first."[19] His rhetoric was no less harsh in his 2011 book *Time to Get Tough*, in which he said, "Illegal immigration is a wrecking ball aimed at U.S. taxpayers."[20] In that book, he also emphasized that he wanted to see a wall built between the United States and Mexico, a theme that he carried into his presidential campaign and presidency.

According to Trump, nothing is ever done about undocumented immigration because powerful forces in the two political parties have a strong interest in maintaining the status
quo: "Too many Republicans in Washington turn a blind
eye to illegal immigration because some of their business
supporters want artificially cheap labor. Liberal Democrats, on
the other hand, look on illegal immigrants as another potential
voting bloc eager for their big government agenda of welfare
handouts, class warfare, and 'affirmative action.'"[21] The Alt-
Right often makes similar arguments.

Even though Trump made immigration a key point
throughout his campaign, he was not entirely consistent on
this subject during his presidential run. In a debate in early
March 2016, Trump hinted that he was softening his position on immigration, stating, "I'm changing, I'm changing."
He went on, "We need highly skilled people in this country.
. . . One of the biggest problems we have is people go to the
best colleges . . . [and] as soon as they're finished, they'll get
shoved out."[22] This seemed at odds with his earlier criticisms
of high-skilled immigration and left viewers confused as to
where he really stood on these issues. The very next day,
Trump seemed to change his tune yet again, restating his
commitment to ending foreign work programs (such as the
H-1B program) that allow companies to hire skilled workers
from abroad.[23]

As president, Trump has mostly maintained his strong anti-
immigration position. He implemented a travel ban from several majority-Muslim countries. He has continued calling for
a physical border wall, though at the time of this writing, this
project has not begun. He also demanded an end to so-called
chain migration, in which immigrants can sponsor members
of their extended families, as well as an end to the diversity
visa lottery, which encourages immigration from countries
that have not traditionally been a major source of immigrants.
All these positions please the Alt-Right, although the massive

reduction in immigration that the movement longed for has not yet materialized.

### Why Was the Alt-Right So Energized by Donald Trump?

Because the Alt-Right was so enthusiastic about the Trump campaign, it is understandable that people made the connection between the movement and Trump. Donald Trump echoed many far-right talking points about immigrants. In the speech that launched his campaign, Trump referred to Mexican immigrants as rapists and criminals. Trump helped normalize anti-immigrant rhetoric that had previously been taboo in conventional presidential politics. Prior to the 2016 presidential primaries, many leading Republicans wanted to distance the party from its restrictionist immigration stance, in the hope that the party could make inroads among Latinos and Asian American voters. Trump destroyed those hopes and reinforced the GOP's reputation as the party of nativism, though it is worth noting that exit polls suggest Trump performed no worse among these demographic groups than Mitt Romney had in 2012.

Donald Trump excited the Alt-Right because of the chaos that he created in Republican politics in 2015 and 2016. Because the Alt-Right despises the conservative movement, they were delighted to see him attack mainstream Republicans and conservative institutions.

Throughout the campaign, Trump retweeted a number of posts from the Alt-Right. To take just one example, he retweeted an image from an account that used the handle "white genocide." He also retweeted an image of Hillary Clinton that stated that she was the "most corrupt candidate ever!" Although the substance of the tweet was congruent with Trump's usual talking points, it was perceived as anti-Semitic because it included a Star of David and originated on a far-right message board. The Trump campaign made race and racism major topics covered in American media. The Alt-Right was able to use these discussions to inject itself into the national conversation.

Throughout the 2016 presidential election, Donald Trump enjoyed enormous enthusiasm from the Alt-Right, and Alt-Right trolls eagerly attacked his critics on social media throughout the campaign. However, most of the leading voices in the Alt-Right also acknowledged that Trump did not share major elements of their ideology.

After Trump won the general election, many in the Alt-Right claimed that they played a pivotal role in his victory, declaring that they "memed him into office."[24] Although this position is difficult to prove one way or the other, one can be skeptical of it. It is just as likely that his opponents' attempts to connect Trump to the Alt-Right cost him more votes than it gained. In the absence of Alt-Right trolls, Trump may have had a more comfortable victory. However, although he may not have benefited from the Alt-Right, the Alt-Right definitely benefited from him. Whether inadvertently or not, the Trump campaign set a new tone for racial discourse in the United States. It restored the radical right to the headlines and the public consciousness, providing it new opportunities to reach out to the public.

### How Has President Trump Responded to His Support from the Alt-Right?

Most observers have been disappointed by President Trump's lackluster efforts to distance himself from the radical right, both during the campaign and afterward. Trump hesitated to repudiate his support from white nationalists such as David Duke, for example.

During the election cycle, he never denounced the Alt-Right, despite repeated calls to do so. He did not finally renounce this part of his base until late November 2016. At the first National Policy Institute (NPI) conference held after the election, Richard Spencer declared, "Hail Trump, hail our people, hail victory," and a number of people in the audience responded with Nazi salutes. This was all captured on video. When confronted with this material, Trump finally said, "I disavow the group."[25]

As president, Trump has taken few steps to distance himself from his supporters in the Alt-Right. He has mostly turned a blind eye to the movement's existence, treating it as something that is not relevant to his agenda. He outraged observers across the globe and the political spectrum when he failed to denounce the Alt-Right after the "Unite the Right" rally in Charlottesville, Virginia, in 2017, for example (see the section "What Were the Consequences of the 'Unite the Right' Rally?" in chapter 6).

### What Does the Alt-Right Think of Donald Trump Today?

Since the inauguration, most voices in the Alt-Right have expressed disappointment in President Trump. In terms of actual policy, he mostly has been a conventional Republican. Although mainstream conservatives were delighted that President Trump appointed a strong conservative—Neil Gorsuch—to the Supreme Court, and that he signed a major tax reform bill, the Alt-Right never really cared about either of those issues. On his signature campaign issue, immigration, Trump accomplished relatively little in his first year in office. There was no significant effort to build a border wall, for example. He suggested many times that he would accept a bill to provide permanent legal status to a class of undocumented immigrants called *Dreamers,* who arrived in the United States as children and have otherwise broken no U.S. laws. His most significant restrictionist policy was a temporary ban on immigrants from several majority-Muslim countries. Although controversial, this policy will have a negligible impact on demographic trends in the United States. The Alt-Right is pleased by Trump's recent calls for decreased legal immigration, but this policy has yet to be implemented and faces an uphill battle in Congress.

The Alt-Right was also outraged by President Trump's decision in 2017 to bomb Syria following revelations that the Assad regime had used chemical weapons on its own people. Following Trump's decision, Richard Spencer led a small Alt-Right protest in front of the White House, in which protesters chanted, "We want walls, not war."[26] They were similarly frustrated when the United States again bombed Syria in 2018. Leading Alt-Right voices feared that this act indicated that Trump's foreign policy would be indistinguishable from that of previous Republicans like George W. Bush. This suspicion was apparently unfounded, however, as the American bombing raid was not a precursor to more significant American interventions in the Syrian civil war.

The Alt-Right has similarly been disappointed by Trump's conventional choices for major White House positions. With a couple of exceptions, Trump's cabinet is full of established Republican leaders. If personnel is policy, then the Trump administration looks similar to other Republican administrations.

Although the Alt-Right has been disappointed in the substance of Trump's presidency, they remain enthusiastic about his style. They have been pleased by his unwillingness to denounce their movement even when it would have been politically expedient to do so. The Alt-Right's proponents share Trump's loathing of mainstream news sources and are pleased that he is delegitimizing them, at least in the eyes of his supporters. They similarly appreciate the degree to which he causes outrage among their political enemies. Although Trump may be, in substance, a conventional Republican president in many ways, he nonetheless is creating higher levels of polarization and distrust, which the Alt-Right hopes to exaggerate and exploit.

## What Was the Significance of Hillary Clinton's "Alt-Right Speech"?

From the Alt-Right's perspective, the Hillary Clinton presidential campaign's decision to call out the movement specifically may have been the most significant event of the election cycle. In August 2016, Clinton gave a speech in Reno, Nevada, in which she linked Donald Trump directly to the Alt-Right. Trump's decision to hire Steve Bannon (see the section "Who Is Steve Bannon?" in chapter 9) a few weeks earlier seems to have been the catalyst for the speech.

Although described as the "Alt-Right speech," it covered many different topics, some unrelated to the movement.[27] She discussed Russian president Vladimir Putin and Nigel Farage of the UK Independence Party (UKIP). She also mentioned conspiracy theorist Alex Jones (see the section "What Is InfoWars?" in chapter 9). The speech's implication was that these groups were part of a larger right-wing nationalist movement, which is somewhat misleading. The speech also praised George W. Bush and John McCain, noting that Donald Trump and his supporters were qualitatively different from previous Republican presidential candidates. The target of the speech seemed to be moderate Republicans who may have already had misgivings about Trump.

Although Clinton lambasted both Trump and the Alt-Right, the Alt-Right was jubilant at the new attention. Alt-Right websites apparently experienced a massive increase in traffic, and the term was suddenly a household name. It dominated the news cycle for several days after the speech and became one of the major stories of the 2016 campaign cycle.

## Are There Alt-Right Sympathizers in the Trump White House?

Despite directly taking on the so-called Republican establishment during the 2016 GOP primaries, the Trump White House mostly picked established Republicans for top positions. To some extent, they had no choice. There was not a large pool of qualified people in Washington who subscribed to Trump's right-wing populist agenda. Nonetheless, some figures within the White House are viewed as more right-wing than the Republican norm. Aside from Trump, three names from the Trump administration most associated with the Alt-Right are Steve Bannon, Stephen Miller, and Sebastian Gorka. I discuss Bannon in greater detail in the section "Who Is Steve Bannon?" in chapter 9.

Miller, a senior policy advisor to the president, is one of the most vocal anti-immigrant figures in the White House. During the presidential campaign, he served in the same function. Miller also has some tangential connections to the Alt-Right. He was an undergraduate at Duke University while Richard Spencer was a graduate student there. The two collaborated to sponsor an immigration debate that included Peter Brimelow, who runs the anti-immigration site *VDARE*. Miller claims, however, that he has had no contact with Spencer in many years, and there is no evidence at this time suggesting otherwise. Miller, who is Jewish, also states that Spencer had no impact on his ideological development.

Gorka, a former deputy assistant to President Trump, has also been accused of having Alt-Right ties. Like Bannon and Miller, Gorka was a right-wing hardliner on immigration and Islam. He was also accused of having connections to a Hungarian neo-Nazi organization. He was forced out of the White House in August 2017, shortly after Bannon's departure.

# 9

# THE ALT-LITE

### *What Is Meant by* Alt-Lite*?*

In 2016, as it became obvious to more observers that the Alt-Right was, at its core, a racist movement dedicated to white identity politics above all other concerns, a new term became part of the public lexicon: *Alt-Lite* (sometimes spelled *Alt-Light*). This term was initially created by the Alt-Right to refer to its less radical fellow travelers. The Alt-Lite often used tactics and talking points that resembled the Alt-Right's, but its major figures typically stopped short of explicit racism.

### *How Is the Alt-Lite Different from the Alt-Right?*

There is not always a hard boundary between the categories of Alt-Right and Alt-Lite, and people can disagree as to how particular groups and individuals should be labeled. Some may question whether we should even make such a distinction. In general, however, these groups tend to differ in the following ways. Compared to the Alt-Right, the Alt-Lite has a much larger audience. At the time of this writing, Richard Spencer has a little under 80,000 followers on Twitter. Most figures in the Alt-Right, including some of the most prominent voices, have far fewer. In contrast, Mike Cernovich, one of the most popular figures that I label as *Alt-Lite*, has over 400,000 followers.

Both the Alt-Lite and the Alt-Right were overwhelmingly supportive of Donald Trump during the 2016 presidential election. Since Trump's inauguration, however, the two groups have diverged in their attitudes toward the president. Most of the Alt-Lite remains enthusiastic about Trump and continues to promote his agenda and attack his opponents. The Alt-Right has expressed more dissatisfaction with Trump on average, noting that there are few ways that his agenda has been congruent with the movement's larger ideological goals, and that he has supported many policies that they oppose.

Both groups are anti-immigration, but the Alt-Lite avoids making explicitly racial arguments about this subject. The Alt-Lite typically makes its case on immigration by focusing on economics or culture. It mostly avoids transparent anti-Semitism and often actually supports Israel. Like the Alt-Right, the Alt-Lite opposes Muslim immigration into Western countries, but they usually frame their arguments differently. The Alt-Lite attacks Islam because of Muslims' purported anti-Semitism and homophobia—issues that do not concern the Alt-Right very much, if at all. The Alt-Right is more likely to point out that most Muslims are racially distinct from Europeans, and that alone is sufficient grounds for exclusion; they would oppose immigration from Syria and Somalia even if the potential immigrants first converted to Christianity or abandoned religion entirely.

The Alt-Lite is more libertarian than the Alt-Right, declaring its unequivocal support for free speech. It considers itself part of the broader classical liberal family, unlike the Alt-Right, which is part of a more radical right-wing tradition.

### What Is the New Right?

Several different ideological groups have adopted the label *New Right*. But this is not a new term. Richard Viguerie and others used it to describe the movement that put Ronald Reagan in office. More radical movements, such as the European New Right (ENR) and North American New Right (NANR), have also used this label. The Alt-Lite is the most recent ideological movement to call itself "New Right." Most figures that I consider part of the Alt-Lite prefer to call themselves "New Right," which is a logical preference, given their recent desire to distinguish themselves from the more extreme Alt-Right.

### What Is Breitbart News?

*Breitbart News* is the media outlet most associated with Donald Trump's right-wing populist movement. The conservative publisher Andrew Breitbart launched the site in 2005. Over time, it became one of the most popular online venues for conservative news and opinion. The site always had a strong populist and confrontational style, frequently deriding so-called political correctness. Although it discussed the same issues as other conservative websites and journals, its adversarial tone made it stand out.

Compared to other outlets for conservative opinion, *Breitbart* was more willing to engage in racial dog-whistling, writing numerous articles on the dangers of black crime, for example. It has also been consistently anti-immigration. The site has faced controversy for cases in which it ran stories that were false or misleading. For instance, *Breitbart* ran a story that supposedly showed Shirley Sherrod, a government official, expressing antiwhite racism in a public forum. She was quickly forced to resign. Shortly thereafter, it was revealed that *Breitbart* had run a deceptively edited video. Because of this controversy, Andrew Breitbart was banned as an on-air guest on the Fox News Channel.[1]

The site moved even further to the right when Andrew Breitbart unexpectedly died at a young age (he was only 43 years old) in 2012. Stephen Bannon joined *Breitbart News* as executive chair immediately afterward. Under Bannon's leadership, *Breitbart* maintained its attacks on mainstream journalists, and its tone became even more explicitly nationalist. Although in substance, its editorial stances differed relatively little from more mainstream conservative venues, its style and rhetoric set it apart. It demanded that Republicans in Congress reject any calls for compromise, and instead to support an ultraconservative, Tea Party economic agenda. It also continued to promote a nativist agenda on immigration. *Breitbart* was among the first major news venues to report on the child migrant crisis in 2014, for example, and did so in an allegedly misleading manner.

As the term *Alt-Right* entered general circulation, it began to be associated with *Breitbart*. This was largely because of Bannon's decision to hire Milo Yiannopoulos (see the section "Who Is Milo Yiannopoulos?" later in this chapter) as a senior editor in 2014. During his tenure at *Breitbart*, Yiannopoulos was the site's most controversial personality. He was also one of the first significant public figures to write a mostly positive article on the Alt-Right. In addition, Yiannopoulos was known for his extreme stances on feminism and Islam.

The other main connection between the Alt-Right and *Breitbart* came from Bannon himself. In 2016, Bannon described *Breitbart* as a "platform of the Alt-Right" to a reporter with *Mother Jones*.[2] This claim was troubling to many people, especially since Bannon made it shortly before he left *Breitbart* and joined the Trump campaign. It gave more fodder to Trump's opponents (both Republican and Democratic), who wished to associate him with the Alt-Right. The claim was also curious because it was not accurate. Although *Breitbart* has always been to the right of more respectable journals of conservative opinion, it had never advocated for explicit white nationalism. Neither did the main venues of Alt-Right opinion on the Internet regularly express admiration for *Breitbart*. However, *Breitbart* could be reasonably labeled as "Alt-Lite."

The subsequent question is why Bannon made this statement, which seems especially odd, given his subsequent disavowal of white nationalism and Richard Spencer. This can probably be explained by the specific context in which he made the statement. For a period in 2015 and 2016, the term *Alt-Right* was being applied widely, often as a generic term for Trump's entire movement, which was always ideologically diverse. Journalist Joshua Green suggested that this was the case in his 2017 book *Devil's Bargain: Steve Bannon, Donald Trump, and the Storming of the Presidency,* on Bannon and the Trump campaign. According to Green:

> The term "alt-right" itself had no fixed meaning. In the broadest sense, it encompassed the spectrum of groups left over if you took everyone to the right of center and subtracted the mainstream Republicans and neoconservative foreign-policy hawks: populists, libertarians, immigration restrictionists, paleoconservatives, and full-on neo-Nazis. This catchall definition is what Bannon had in mind.[3]

Regardless of Bannon's intention when he made the statement, the connections between Bannon, *Breitbart*, Trump, and the Alt-Right are now fixed in many people's minds. Following the election, *Breitbart* attempted to reinvent itself as a serious source of conservative journalism. It hired several respected journalists once associated with mainstream venues such as *The Hill, RealClearPolitics,* and the *Wall Street Journal.*

*Breitbart* remains a major source of populist right-wing material. Bannon returned to his leadership position at the site after he was dismissed from the Trump administration, only to lose it again at the beginning of 2018.

### Who Is Steve Bannon?

Steve Bannon is best known as the chief executive of Trump's presidential campaign, and later as the White House chief strategist. Before entering the political arena, he had had a successful career in the military and business. He served as a naval officer and later earned an MBA from Harvard and worked for Goldman Sachs. Bannon also had a stint in Hollywood, where he worked as an executive producer. Part of his wealth derives from his stake in the television program *Seinfeld*, which still provides him a source of revenue whenever the show is aired.

Bannon can be described as Islamophobic. He developed his ideas about Muslims during his time in the U.S. navy. He was tangentially involved in the Jimmy Carter administration's disastrous attempt to rescue hostages from the U.S. embassy in Iran following the Iranian Revolution.

Bannon became the chief executive of the Trump campaign in August 2016. His presence on the campaign was controversial, providing further evidence that Trump was friendly with the Alt-Right. Whereas other Republicans hoped that Trump would moderate his tone after securing the GOP nomination, Bannon encouraged Trump to maintain his right-wing populist platform and his unrelenting attacks on Hillary Clinton.

Bannon followed Trump to the White House, where he was appointed chief strategist. He also briefly served on the National Security Council. He apparently played a role in drafting the executive order that barred immigration from seven majority-Muslim countries. Many observers perceived Bannon as an important player in the White House, pushing Trump to implement his nationalist agenda. His influence may have been overstated, however. When we look at the ideological leanings of the Trump administration, Bannon was always an outlier. Aside from Bannon, Stephen Miller, Sebastian Gorka, Michael Anton, and perhaps Attorney General Jeff Sessions (who was an outspoken immigration restrictionist during his time in the U.S. Senate), most of Trump's appointees were conventional Republicans, and it also is not clear that Bannon had a disproportionate influence over policy.

Regardless of his real level of influence, Bannon did not long serve in the administration. He apparently feuded with other important figures in the White House, including the president's son-in-law, Jared Kushner. It was rumored that Bannon was the source of several anonymous and embarrassing leaks. He departed the White House in August 2017, shortly after the "Unite the Right" rally in Charlottesville. Although Bannon's relationship with the president had been deteriorating for some time, he had apparently become too much of a political liability.

After leaving the administration, Bannon returned to *Breitbart*. He then further denounced the Alt-Right, reiterating that he was an economic nationalist, but he opposed racial nationalism. Bannon claimed that he would continue to support Trump and his movement from outside the White House, but he quickly began taking positions at odds with Trump. For example, he supported the controversial judge Roy Moore for the Alabama special election to the U.S. Senate, whereas Trump supported the more conventional Republican Luther Strange. Moore won the primary, but he subsequently lost the general election to the Democratic candidate, Doug Jones, largely due to accusations that Moore had engaged in inappropriate sexual behavior several decades earlier. The result was a disaster for Republicans, who lost a senate seat in one of the most Republican states in the country, and it became an embarrassment for Bannon.

Bannon faced new problems in late 2017, when the journalist Michael Wolff reported in his book, *Fire and Fury: Inside the Trump White House*, that he had described a meeting between Donald Trump, Jr. and other campaign officials and a Russian lawyer in 2016 as "treasonous."[4] Trump subsequently denounced Bannon. More significantly, he was also fired from *Breitbart*.

Prior to these challenges, Bannon had expressed hope that he would be able to assist right-wing challengers in GOP primaries in the run-up to the 2018 midterm elections. Given his recent difficulties, it appears unlikely that Bannon will again be a major player in U.S. partisan politics in the near future.

### Who Is Milo Yiannopoulos?

In 2016, Milo Yiannopoulos was one of the most famous figures associated with the Alt-Right, even though he never used the term as a self-description. He is best known for his writings at *Breitbart*, where he was an editor from 2015 until 2017. Yiannopoulos may seem like an odd figure to be associated with a white nationalist movement, given his own demographic characteristics. He is a half-Jewish gay man married to an African American man. However, he is also a right-wing provocateur, best known for his attacks on Islam, feminism, and transgendered people. He has also made many anti-immigrant remarks, and he was a staunch Trump supporter in the 2016 presidential election.

Yiannopoulos wrote one of the first articles on the Alt-Right for a major news outlet, an essay titled "An Establishment Conservative's Guide to the Alt-Right," published at *Breitbart* in early 2016.[5] Although much of what the essay said was factually correct, it was also misleading. It argued, for example, that white nationalist ideologues represented just a small element of the Alt-Right, and that the movement was largely a reaction to stifling political correctness. More than a year after Yiannopoulos published that article, a series of leaked e-mails showed that the essay was deliberately misleading, and that Yiannopoulos had collaborated with white nationalists when writing it.[6]

Aside from his writings at *Breitbart*, Yiannopoulos is known for giving provocative speeches on college campuses, making outrageous statements like "Feminism is cancer." His campus tours were often the catalysts for major protests, some of them violent. When Yiannopoulos came to the University of California at Berkeley in early 2017 at the invitation of the College Republicans, protesters with Antifa (see the section "What Is Antifa?" in chapter 10) disrupted the event, causing its cancellation. The protests continued even after the cancellation, however, causing significant property damage.

Yiannopoulos developed a significant following on Twitter and was a well-known troll (see the section, "What Is a Troll?" in chapter 5). This ended when comments that he directed at the African American actor and comedian Leslie Jones caused her to face a barrage of racist vitriol from the Alt-Right. Twitter subsequently banned him from the platform.

At the start of 2017, Yiannopoulos's career seemed to be on an upward trajectory. He had distanced himself from the more radical elements of the Alt-Right and expressed his contempt for all forms of identity politics—leading to a wave of denunciations from the Alt-Right, but building his credibility among more mainstream conservatives. He signed a lucrative book deal and was scheduled to speak at the Conservative Political Action Conference (CPAC), the conservative movement's most important annual gathering.

This all fell apart, however, when some of Yiannopoulos's earlier remarks, which seemed to justify and even glorify pederasty, became widely known. His CPAC speech was cancelled, as was his book deal. He also lost his job at *Breitbart*. Yiannopoulos subsequently had to self-publish his memoir, *Dangerous*. He continues to write and post videos at his new website, dangerous.com. He also continues to go on speaking tours. However, his public profile has significantly diminished.

### Who Is Mike Cernovich?

Mike Cernovich is a well-known blogger and author with a large social media presence. His work has not always been political. For some time, he was best known for his self-published book *Gorilla Mindset*, a self-help book. His website, *Danger and Play*, has a significant amount of nonpolitical material, much of it focused on gender relations. His site was part of the broader "manosphere" (see the section "What Is the Men's Rights Movement?" in chapter 4). He also promoted Gamergate (see the section "What Is Gamergate?" in chapter 4).

Cernovich became increasingly political over the course of the 2016 election, and his site and Twitter feed focused heavily on supporting Trump. He also produced a documentary film called *Silenced,* which discussed the "war on free speech." The film included several people associated with the Alt-Right or Alt-Lite, but it also included interviews with mainstream figures such as legal scholar Alan Dershowitz. He was also one of the main promoters of the so-called Pizzagate conspiracy theories—the discredited theory that major Democratic leaders and Hillary Clinton allies operated a secret child-sex ring.

Throughout 2016, Cernovich seemed to have good relationships with major figures in the Alt-Right, and rhetoric in his Twitter feed mimicked much of what one finds on the Alt-Right. He sometimes used the term "we" when discussing the Alt-Right.[7] This relationship became much more strained following the 2016 election, however. Cernovich disinvited Alt-Right figures from the postelection "Deploraball," which he organized to celebrate Trump's election victory. The event's name was a reference to Hillary Clinton's earlier remark about Trump's supporters including a "basket of deplorables." He also became a more vocal critic of figures like Richard Spencer, accusing him of being "controlled opposition," and perhaps even a federal agent working to undermine the political right.[8]

### Who Is Gavin McInnes, and Who Are The Proud Boys?

The Canadian-born Gavin McInnes is best known as the cofounder of *Vice* magazine. He left the magazine in 2008. McInnes also cofounded an advertising agency and worked in film and radio. He maintains a stereotypical hipster persona and uses humor when making his political and cultural arguments.

McInnes has long been open about his right-wing views. He wrote four articles for the anti-immigration site *VDARE* in 2005, for example. However, he became more vocal on political questions after leaving *Vice*. His has written for several publications affiliated with the Alt-Right. He contributed an article to *American Renaissance* in 2014. He also writes a column for *Taki's Magazine*, and began writing for that venue when Richard Spencer was still its editor.

Despite these controversial affiliations, McInnes has many connections with more mainstream conservative media. He was a contributor to Fox News for eight years, though he ended his relationship with the channel in early 2017. He was also one of the most popular commentators at *The Rebel*, a Canadian right-wing website, though he also broke ties with that venue in 2017. Aside from McInnes, *The Rebel* has employed several other figures whose views may be described as Alt-Right or Alt-Lite, including Lauren Southern, conspiracy theorist and pro-Trump political activist Jack Posobiec, and far-right Canadian political commentator Faith Goldy. A right-wing media company called Conservative Review currently employs McInnes. Their website also hosts programs by conservative commentators such as Mark Levin and Michelle Malkin.

McInnes has never described himself as a white nationalist, and he is married to a nonwhite woman and has mixed-race children. His most controversial writings have focused on questions of gender and sexuality. He has expressed hostility to feminism and disgust toward transgendered people. He describes himself as a libertarian, but he supported Donald Trump in the 2016 presidential election and supports immigration restrictions.

Although not as extreme as the major figures associated with the Alt-Right, McInnes is nonetheless controversial. Protesters disrupted a speech that he attempted to give at New York University, pepper-spraying him and forcing the event's cancellation.

McInnes recently denounced the Alt-Right. He describes his own ideology as "Western chauvinism," which maintains that Western culture is objectively superior to others. The difference between this view and white nationalism, according to McInnes and others who share this view, is that Western chauvinists maintain that nonwhites can be part of Western culture. He critiques the Alt-Right for its single-minded focus on race rather than other considerations, and he also expresses support for Israel.

The Proud Boys is a fraternal organization often categorized as part of the Alt-Right. McInnes founded the group in 2016. It is not officially a political organization of any sort and does not campaign for candidates or raise money for political causes. On its website, it openly describes itself as an "Alt-Lite" organization. To my knowledge, it is the only group that uses that term as a self-description.

The Proud Boys has many strange rules and hazing rituals, more closely resembling a college fraternity than a political group. Moving up in "degrees" in The Proud Boys requires several steps. To be a first-degree Proud Boy, one must only publicly state that he is a Proud Boy. To be a second-degree Proud Boy, one must agree to stop masturbating and recite the names of five breakfast cereals while being punched by other Proud Boys. Third-degree Proud Boys are required to get a Proud Boy tattoo.

Although McInnes insists that it is an apolitical group primarily focused on socializing and drinking beer, The Proud Boys has earned a reputation for violence because its members have routinely clashed with antiracist protesters. They have a "tactical defensive arm" called the Fraternal Order of the Alt-Knights, headed by a political activist named Kyle Chapman, who became well known after being filmed fighting with Antifa protesters.[9]

*The Proud Boys* website includes many articles on culture written from a right-wing perspective. Proud Boys material also uses words typically associated with the Alt-Right. It has a regular feature called "Cuck of the Week," for example. The Southern Poverty Law Center labels The Proud Boys as a hate group.

Although there are some ideological affinities between The Proud Boys and the Alt-Right, McInnes has sought recently to put even greater distance between his group and white nationalists. For example, Proud Boys are now forbidden to take part in Alt-Right rallies or other activities. The Proud Boys also emphasizes that it is a racially diverse group, allowing both Jews and gays to join the organization.

### What Is InfoWars?

The conspiracy theorist Alex Jones owns the website *Infowars*, which hosts Jones's show and other radical materials. The website promotes conspiracy theories, such as that the Sandy Hook massacre was a hoax and that the 9/11 attacks were perpetrated by the U.S. government. Like Mike Cernovich (see the section "Who Is Mike Cernovich?" earlier in this chapter), Jones endorsed the Pizzagate conspiracy theory. He also promotes conspiracy theories about "the new world order" and insists that "globalists" have a secret plan to enslave humanity.

Jones and others associated with *Infowars*, such as Paul Joseph Watson, are often associated with the Alt-Right. The conspiratorial content at *InfoWars* is not especially racist or anti-Semitic, although among anti-Semites, *globalist* is often used as a code word for Jews. Jones was recently accused of making anti-Semitic and racist statements in the workplace, though he denies these claims.[10] Few in the Alt-Right claim Jones or Watson as part of their movement, and neither of these men claims to be Alt-Right. Watson has described himself as "New Right."

### What Is the Relationship Between the Alt-Lite and the Alt-Right?

Over the last few years, the Alt-Right's opinion of the less radical Alt-Lite has evolved. For much of the 2016 election, there was little fighting between the Alt-Right and the Alt-Lite. Most of the Alt-Right viewed the Alt-Lite as a way to introduce people to nationalist ideas, with the hope that eventually they would embrace more radical views. There were some exceptions to this. Andrew Anglin, for example, was always a critic of Milo Yiannopoulos and others in the Alt-Lite.

The relationship became strained following President Trump's victory. The more moderate voices in the Alt-Lite, who hoped to transition into a mainstream political force, sought to distance themselves from white nationalists. This increased after the National Policy Institute (NPI) conference in 2016 where many Alt-Right followers were filmed making Nazi salutes. The break became more formal when Alt-Lite personalities such as Mike Cernovich organized the "Deploraball." Cernovich made it clear that Richard Spencer and his supporters were not welcome at the event. The Alt-Right also became increasingly critical of the Alt-Lite around this time. Social media feuds between the two camps became common.

Following the 2016 presidential election, most people who did not describe themselves as white nationalists stopped describing themselves as Alt-Right. People such as Yiannopoulos, Cernovich, and McInnes have stated their opposition to ethnonationalism and anti-Semitism, though they do not disavow their anti-immigration views or Islamophobia. The break has clarified that the Alt-Right is a movement of white nationalists, and people uncomfortable with that ideology have broken away. The Alt-Right has responded by describing the Alt-Lite as weak and timid, possessing no coherent ideology.

In early 2017, the Alt-Right and Alt-Lite held competing rallies on the same day in Washington, D.C. The Alt-Right "free speech" rally, which included Spencer and other white nationalists such as Jason Kessler and Nathan Damigo, was held at the Lincoln Memorial. The Alt-Lite "Rally Against Political Violence" took place near the White House. The Alt-Lite rally included speakers such as Cernovich and Jack Posobiec. When asked about the Alt-Lite rally, Spencer declared, "They're ultimately bad people. I mean if you meet Jack Posobiec, Mike Cernovich, they're just liars, they're con artists, they're freaks. They're not the people we want to be associated with."[11]

### Does the Alt-Lite Help the Alt-Right?

Throughout 2016, many on the Alt-Right were hopeful that their less radical fellow travelers would serve as a gateway to their ideology. Although people may not be willing to make an immediate jump from a mainstream ideology to white nationalism, the thinking was that if readers spent some time consuming Alt-Lite material, they might become more accepting of explicit white nationalism and eventually move further to the right. At this point, no one has quantitatively studied the process by which people embraced the Alt-Right's ideology. For that reason, there is no way to discern whether that intuition was correct. In order for these transitions to occur, however, there needed to be amicable relationships between the two camps and overlap among their followers. This was definitely the case in 2015 and 2016. It is not clear that it is still true.

Following the many acrimonious public disputes between the Alt-Right and Alt-Lite, the dividing lines are now clearer. As a result, it is less likely that the Alt-Right is drawing a significant number of new converts from the Alt-Lite. In fact, the Alt-Lite may actually be a hindrance to the Alt-Right's growth at this point. Figures in the Alt-Lite are radical in their own ways, and to various degrees, but they are less extreme than the Alt-Right. Rather than being a mere bridge between the conservative movement and the Alt-Right, the Alt-Lite may be a long-lasting alternative to both of those ideologies. On the other hand, it has faced many setbacks of its own since 2016, and it may wither as a political force, making this question moot.

# 10

# COMBATING THE ALT-RIGHT

### What Is Doxing?

*Doxing* means releasing a person's personal information that otherwise is not publicly available. This can take the form of exposing the true identity of someone who was previously anonymous online, or publishing the phone number, address, or other contact information of someone whose identity is already known. Both the Alt-Right and its opponents engage in doxing.

When the Alt-Right doxes someone, it is usually meant as a form of intimidation. When the movement identifies someone as an enemy—usually a journalist or activist—releasing his or her private contact information can lead to that person receiving threatening e-mails, phone calls, or letters. It is uncommon for the Alt-Right to expose the real identity of an anonymous person, as most of its main opponents are open about their identities.

Doxing the Alt-Right usually means exposing the identity of someone who would prefer to stay anonymous. Because open expressions of white nationalism remain mostly taboo in the United States, many people associated with the Alt-Right prefer to keep their real names a secret. This allows them to engage in far-right activism without risking their jobs or personal relationships.

Over the last several years, a growing number of Alt-Right figures have been doxed, often causing them serious personal problems. For example, doxers exposed the popular Alt-Right YouTube personality who uses the name "Millennial Woes" in late 2016. Around that same time, the proprietor of *The Right Stuff*, who uses the name "Mike Enoch," was doxed, as were some other people associated with the website. This doxing was particularly dramatic, as it disrupted Enoch's personal life—causing the end of his marriage and the loss of his job— but it also caused him to lose esteem among many people within the Alt-Right. The revelation of Enoch's real identity also exposed the fact that he was married to a Jewish woman, which was shocking given his long history of vulgar anti- Semitism. This case of doxing caused significant disruptions at *The Right Stuff*. Most notably, the hosts of the popular podcast *Fash the Nation*, broadcast on the site, stopped producing new episodes, even though they had not personally been doxed. The show resumed several months later.

Doxing does not typically require a high level of techno- logical sophistication. It usually involves following clues that a person left behind somewhere on the Internet. As a person becomes better known, doxing becomes increasingly likely to the point of inevitability. Millennial Woes, for example, never revealed his real name in any of his videos, but he never made any attempt to hide his face. As he became one of the more fa- mous Alt-Right figures on the Internet, it was only a matter of time before someone recognized him in the real world.

Other doxings occur because of carelessness, such as linking a supposedly anonymous social media account with one's personal e-mail address or a different social media account containing personal information. One can now find articles explaining best practices in "operational security" at some Alt- Right venues. That is, they describe steps one can take to better conceal their real identities.

There was another wave of doxing after the "Unite the Right" rally. Hundreds of people marching with the Alt-Right were caught on camera, and after the event was over, journalists and antiracist activists sifted through the pictures and attempted to uncover the identities of the people who were pictured. Some of these efforts were crowdsourced over social media. As a result, many people were identified and subsequently lost their jobs or faced threats of expulsion from their universities.

There have also been occasions where people within the Alt-Right have doxed each other because of ideological or personal disputes. Doxing a fellow right-winger is considered an extreme taboo within those circles, but because it is comparatively easy to set up an anonymous website or post anonymously on 4chan or 8chan, one can engage in that kind of behavior with little fear of retaliation.

### Is Doxing Effective?

It may not be immediately obvious what doxing is supposed to achieve. It is true that affiliation with the radical right can cause a person severe problems, loss of employment being perhaps the most significant. However, after a person has been doxed, he or she has little incentive to give up involvement in the far right. In fact, after losing other relationships and sources of income, the radical right may be the only source of social and financial support a person has left. Millennial Woes did not stop producing videos after being doxed. After a short disruption, *The Right Stuff* began producing more content than before the doxing, and Enoch became a more prominent figure in the Alt-Right, showing up publicly at multiple events in the following year. With every case of doxing, there is a risk that the affected person will become more active in the movement.

However, focusing just on the most high-profile doxing cases may not reveal the entire story. The primary target for doxing may not be the actual victim, but other people who may consider taking part in Alt-Right-related activities. Examples of people with ruined lives because of doxing may cause others to think twice before creating online content or attending a rally. It may similarly cause someone who is already involved in the movement to withdraw out of fear.

When a figure in the Alt-Right is doxed and faces subsequent financial hardship, the movement often works to assist the person. In some cases, the person may even be able to find employment as an Alt-Right activist or content creator. These are rare exceptions, however. The Alt-Right has very few resources of its own, and it has not developed a strong fundraising apparatus; thus, it is not able to sustain more than a handful of people as full-time activists, nor provide very much substantive support for people who face financial difficulties.

Doxing carries the risk of false positives. Volunteer Internet sleuths looking over picture of rallies trying to identify individuals can make mistakes. There have been cases of people falsely accused of taking part in an Alt-Right activity, leading to unwarranted threats and harassment.

### What Is No-Platforming?

*No-platforming* (also called *deplatforming*) refers to efforts to deny venues to certain speakers and ideas. In many developed countries, national governments do this with strong laws against hate speech. The United States is different because the First Amendment protects most kinds of speech, and even the most extreme ideologies are free to spread their message, so long as they do not make explicit and specific calls for violence.

For many years, private businesses have turned away white nationalist groups that sought to hold public events. *American Renaissance* was forced to cancel its conferences in both 2010 and 2011 after it was unable to find a hotel willing to host them. The anti-immigration website *VDARE* has had similar problems finding a place to host its conferences.

One of the ironies of recent no-platforming pushes is that, because the Constitution guarantees the right to free speech, the Alt-Right has increasingly turned to the government that it hates to find venues to publicly express its ideas. Whereas hotels and other private venues can discriminate because of ideas, the government is precluded from doing so. Indeed, civil liberties groups such as the American Civil Liberties Union (ACLU) have a long record of successfully defending racists' right to use public spaces. For this reason, the National Policy Institute (NPI) has hosted most of its conferences in the Ronald Reagan Building in Washington, D.C., and *American Renaissance* held its recent conferences at Montgomery Bell State Park in Tennessee. Richard Spencer has also given many speeches at public universities, and Matthew Heimbach of the Traditionalist Worker Party (TWP) has given speeches on college campuses.

Because the Alt-Right remains predominantly an online phenomenon, however, access to public spaces is arguably less important to the movement than access to Internet services. For its first few years, the Alt-Right was able to work online with little interference or oversight. This is beginning to change. In recent years, the Alt-Right and related groups have been denied access to certain online services.

Throughout 2017, tech corporations increasingly sought to deny the Alt-Right access to their services. For instance, PayPal deleted the accounts of *AltRight.com*, the NPI, *American Renaissance,* Identity Evropa, and several other groups and websites. This caused the movement significant headaches, as the Alt-Right conducts most of its fundraising on the Internet and PayPal is the most popular tool for making online payments. Amazon similarly deleted affiliate accounts for several Alt-Right groups. The Amazon affiliate program is a system whereby people who direct traffic to Amazon receive a portion of every sale made during a single visit. This service once provided meaningful income to various Alt-Right websites. Reddit deleted the r/altright subreddit, which was once among the most popular Alt-Right forums.

The most dramatic case of no-platforming occurred after the "Unite the Right" rally, when the major web hosting platforms sought to push *The Daily Stormer* (see the section "Who Is Andrew Anglin, and What Is *The Daily Stormer?*" in chapter 5) off the Internet entirely. GoDaddy cancelled the site's domain registration, and Cloudflare cancelled its distributed denial of service (DDOS) protection. Google also banned the site from its domain registration. The site jumped from one domain to another in different countries, briefly finding hosts in countries such as Russia, Albania, and Iceland. After each ban, it ceases to be viewable on ordinary web browsers and can only be accessed from the browser Tor.

### Are There Any Risks to No-Platforming?

Many people, including some who oppose the Alt-Right, have raised objections to no-platforming. Denying people the right to express opinions, even opinions that most Americans consider loathsome, violates the classical liberal value of free speech, and raises the specter of McCarthyism and other eras in American history when ideas were driven from the public sphere.

Although private entities, rather than the government, are not required to allow anyone to speak on their property or broadcast or publish from their platforms, private censorship raises additional concerns. The Internet is now one of the world's main channels of communication. We can reasonably question whether it is wise to allow giant corporations like Google or Amazon to be the primary gatekeepers to speech. Although antiracists on the left may applaud these entities for their efforts to crack down on hate speech, it is worth noting that this same tactic can be used on other forms of speech, including left-wing speech, with a similar lack of public oversight. We may not wish to set the precedent that corporations get to determine what kinds of speech can appear online.

### What Is Alt-Tech?

Faced with increasing online challenges, elements of the Alt-Right began creating their own platforms, independent from the major tech companies. The Alt-Right calls this initiative *Alt-Tech*. By creating new and independent platforms, they hope to protect themselves from public pressure to block their propaganda efforts.

One early example of this was a new social media platform called Gab, which from the outset declared its commitment to free speech. Unlike Twitter, Gab very rarely suspends users or deletes their accounts. Many Alt-Right supporters who were banned from Twitter subsequently started using Gab. Some people use both platforms.

Although Gab has weaker rules regarding harassment and hate speech than Twitter, it is also a less effective tool for the Alt-Right. Twitter is valuable for the Alt-Right because it allows the movement to engage with people who are not already followers. Trolling and propaganda campaigns need to be able to reach a major audience to be effective. If Gab remains predominantly a social media platform for the extreme right, it will not be very useful in that regard.

The Alt-Right has also started creating new crowdfunding sites now that it increasingly finds itself cut off from sites like GoFundMe and Patreon. Sites such as Hatreon and GoyFundMe were created to provide similar services to major figures in the Alt-Right—at the time of this writing, however, both of these sites are down. The Alt-Right's loss of access to payment-processing services like PayPal also creates significant problems for sustaining activism, and for that reason, some sites encourage making donations via cryptocurrencies like Bitcoin.

Creating independent domain registrars like GoDaddy remains, for now, beyond the capabilities of Alt-Tech. This is because creating such services requires more than mere technological skill—it also requires an enormous amount of capital, far beyond what the Alt-Right presently enjoys. This has yet to be a major problem for the Alt-Right overall, however. To date, *The Daily Stormer* remains the only significant Alt-Right website that has had great difficulty finding a domain registrar.

In the end, Alt-Tech initiatives may prove to be enormously beneficial to the Alt-Right, giving them a new degree of freedom to operate on the Internet. For now, however, the no-platforming efforts have created major problems for the movement, forcing it to sink considerable time and resources into resolving technical problems rather than engaging in activism and outreach.

### What about Efforts That Try to Persuade Individuals to Leave Hate Groups?

Some efforts to weaken hate groups focus on the individual, working with people ensconced in these networks who wish to get out. Life After Hate is the most significant group that follows this strategy. Co-founded by Christian Picciolini, a former skinhead recruiter, the organization helps people who wish to escape hate groups and build new lives. It runs a program called ExitUSA that works with individuals who want to transition out of such groups, and it has many success stories.

It is unclear whether such efforts can be effective against the Alt-Right, as it is qualitatively different from other kinds of far-right groups. Whereas earlier hate groups were organized like criminal gangs or religious cults, the Alt-Right does not have many "members" in the same sense. Members of the National Socialist Movement (NSM) and skinhead gangs build their relationships and social identities around their membership in the group. People who spend any significant time with such organizations may be covered in racist tattoos that proclaim their affiliations. They are likely be completely cut off from friends and family members who do not share their beliefs. Even if someone begins to question the ideology and violence of the group, that person, if deeply embedded in such an organization, may have limited employment opportunities or outside social support.

The Alt-Right does not operate in a similar manner. There are formal, membership-based Alt-Right groups, such as Identity Evropa, but for now, the movement remains a mostly anonymous, online rabble. The Alt-Right is mostly just people who read blogs, watch videos, and listen to podcasts. When not privately sitting at a computer, people in the Alt-Right may be leading otherwise normal lives. This may change, and elements of the Alt-Right are seeking to build a stronger and more organized real-world network. If they are successful, then efforts to persuade people to leave such groups, and to give them access to resources if they choose to do so, may be very useful. In the meantime, however, these kinds of efforts are less likely to be a major hindrance to the Alt-Right.

### What Is Antifa?

As was the case with the Alt-Right, few Americans were familiar with Antifa (short for *antifascist*) at the start of 2016. However, as the Alt-Right became more prominent and willing to enter public spaces, Antifa groups began showing up in large numbers to challenge them. Although most Americans became aware of Antifa groups only recently, they have a long history. Militant antifascism is as old as fascism itself.

Based on the name, one might infer that Antifa is defined entirely by what it opposes. That is, it is against fascism, but it offers no specific alternative. Although it contains diverse philosophical components, Antifa does have an ideological core. It is a movement of the revolutionary left. Most of its supporters identify with a socialist or left-anarchist ideology. Although their primary concern is combating fascism, Antifa groups are also opposed to the prevailing neoliberal global order and would like to see it replaced.

Antifa is controversial because it openly rejects the classical liberal value of free speech. When Alt-Right and related groups plan public rallies, Antifa groups organize to disrupt them. They disagree with groups like the ACLU, which defend the right of extreme racists to hold public rallies. Antifa groups respond to the charge that they are opposed to free speech by noting that there are already many constraints on free speech; incarcerated people have speech restrictions, for example, and there are laws against obscenity and inciting violence. These groups point out that it is hypocritical for mainstream liberals and conservatives to claim to be free speech purists when it comes to neo-Nazis, yet remain silent on these other issues.

The general Antifa stance on free speech is that protecting marginalized communities and keeping fascists from gaining power are more important than an abstract liberal value, which is already only partially protected in the United States. If keeping fascism from becoming a serious threat requires violating fascists' rights, they argue, it is a small price to pay. After all, fascists in power have historically done far worse than deny people their own right to speak. They furthermore argue that the police and other government institutions cannot be trusted to safeguard the well-being of marginalized communities, which means that antiracist, antifascist organizations must take on this role themselves.

Like the Alt-Right, Antifa is not a unified, hierarchical organization. Many autonomous groups, both large and small, adopt the label. The Black Bloc is the most controversial element of the Antifa movement, as it is the most willing to take violent action against the Alt-Right and similar movements. People who belong to this element of Antifa typically wear black clothing and masks to protect their identities. Black Bloc organizers were responsible for shutting down a Milo Yiannopoulos speech at the University of California, Berkeley, in early 2017. This group was also present at Donald Trump's inauguration, and hundreds were arrested for acts of vandalism and other forms of violence. An apparent Black Bloc member (whose identity remains unknown) famously punched Richard Spencer in the face, an event that was caught on camera and subsequently went viral on social media.

Although the Alt-Right loathes Antifa, people who identify with mainstream ideologies have criticized the movement as well. Most of these attacks have come from conservatives, some of whom have dubbed Antifa the *Alt-Left*, to create the impression that Antifa and the Alt-Right are just two sides of the same extremist coin. People in the center and even on the left also have criticized Antifa, arguing that they not only violate basic liberal principles, but they allow Alt-Right supporters to portray themselves as victims, and thus garner more sympathy. According to this argument, it is better to let racists speak, but respond with larger, peaceful protests. Antifa leaders respond that this weak response to fascist organizing demonstrates historical illiteracy, noting that fascism can quickly grow into an unstoppable force if it is not quashed at its early stages.

Beyond counterprotesting, Antifa groups work to dox people associated with the Alt-Right and infiltrate Alt-Right groups. They also engage in other forms of community organizing. The major Antifa websites emphasize that violence is not the only, or even the primary, activity that they engage in. For a useful introduction to the history and tactics of Antifa, I recommend Mark Bray's book, *Antifa: The Anti-Fascist Handbook*.

### Are Lawsuits an Effective Tool Against the Extreme Right?

Historically, lawsuits have been responsible for undermining some of the most prominent white nationalist organizations. Groups like the Southern Poverty Law Center have a long history of taking on the radical right in civil trials, often successfully. In 1994, it brought a civil lawsuit against the Church of the Creator (CoTC) on behalf of the family of a man who was murdered by a leader of the group. The family was awarded $1 million. The CoTC sought to avoid surrendering its compound to the family by selling it to William Pierce shortly before the lawsuit occurred, but another lawsuit forced Pierce to relinquish the money he earned when he subsequently re-sold it. This was not the end of the CoTC, as it subsequently reorganized under new leadership, but it was weakened. The Southern Poverty Law Center also helped bring down Aryan Nations. When guards at the Aryan Nations compound chased down and assaulted two people who had simply driven near it, the organization was sued by the victims and was ordered to pay a $4.8 million settlement. This forced Aryan Nations to sell their compound, dealing it a fatal blow. At the time of this writing, there is also a pending lawsuit against Richard Spencer, Jason Kessler, Matthew Heimbach, and other people responsible for organizing the "Unite the Right" rally. The plaintiffs in that case are arguing that the defendants conspired to commit violence in Charlottesville.

Even if lawsuits are ultimately unsuccessful, they are a major nuisance to the Alt-Right. Time that its leaders would otherwise spend recruiting and propagandizing is instead spent defending themselves in court. In addition, civil and criminal trials put a major strain on the movement's limited re-sources. But it is unclear whether the lawsuit model can be ap-plied successfully against the Alt-Right, if success is defined as bringing its activities to a halt. Although some people inspired by Alt-Right material have engaged in real-world criminal ac-tivity, the Alt-Right has not engaged in systematic campaigns of real-world violence thus far. The movement is mostly not membership based at this point; it has little in the way of or-ganization and formal hierarchy. Thus, it is harder to demon-strate culpability when these violent acts occur.

Being a racist troll on the Internet is not a crime. Some Alt-Right trolls may have crossed the boundary into criminal ha-rassment, but bringing such people to justice is a challenge because threats often come in the form of anonymous e-mails. More frequently, Alt-Right attacks are simply insults made on websites, forums, and social media. Although people who are on the receiving end of these slurs and abuses can be justifiably disturbed and unnerved, they do not have legal recourse in such instances. If the Alt-Right remains a mostly anonymous online mob, there is little that the law can do to stop it. However, lawsuits and criminal trials may prove a challenge to the Alt-Right as it tries to become more organized.

This effectiveness of courts to stop the Alt-Right will largely depend on the degree to which future Alt-Right institutions resemble their White Nationalism 1.0 predecessors. Figures like Ben Klassen openly yearned for a race war and recruited people with a clear propensity for violence and other antisocial activities. When their followers brought their rhetoric into the real world, there was a clear case against them. For now, most major Alt-Right figures choose their words carefully, and even when they make statements that imply support for violence, they are often spoken or written in an ironic tone, allowing them to plausibly claim that they are only joking or trolling.

### How Worried Should We Really Be?

There is no single strategy that will be a panacea against the Alt-Right. The far right has a track record of adapting to new situations and eventually recovering from major setbacks. I do not expect the Alt-Right to simply disappear. Nonetheless, at the time of this writing, the Alt-Right is declining. Its halcyon days of 2015 and 2016, when it was riding Trump's coattails and drawing new adherents, already seem like a distant memory. The Alt-Right is no longer discussed as a tech-savvy band of meme warriors, skillfully warping young minds and converting a new generation of white nationalists. It is increasingly viewed as a rowdy group of violent thugs, staging stunts designed to draw media attention. The difference between the Alt-Right and those failed white nationalist groups that it sought to replace is becoming less obvious.

The Alt-Right is being challenged on every front. In terms of real-world activism, it is consistently outnumbered and outorganized by those who reject its message. Wherever it goes, it faces great masses of counterprotesters. Because of the dangers involved with real-world far-right activism, especially doxing, the Alt-Right's hope of drawing great crowds of normal-looking people may never be realized. If it wants to stage events in public places without being overwhelmed and drowned out by counterprotesters, it must choose remote locations, where it will be even more difficult to attract their own people and where the media presence (and thus the larger audience) will be limited.

The Alt-Right's ability to organize is increasingly compromised by the steady stream of leaks from its own conversations. For example, much of the planning for "Unite the Right" occurred on the chap app, Discord, which was initially created as a service for video gamers. Following "Unite the Right," many of these conversations were made public by infiltrators. Discord subsequently banned several Alt-Right servers. To my knowledge, the Alt-Right has yet to find a new platform that will allow a large number of people to coordinate their activities discreetly, meaning that its ability to plan large-scale action is increasingly limited.

The Alt-Right is also having problems organizing in the real world, face to face, given the number of people seeking to infiltrate and expose the movement, often successfully. For example, the organization Hope Not Hate managed to embed an infiltrator in the Alt-Right for over a year, attending several private and public Alt-Right events, and secretly recording prominent Alt-Right figures. These kinds of events create an atmosphere of distrust, making it increasingly difficult for the Alt-Right to organize private events.

No-platforming efforts have undermined the Alt-Right's ability to operate on the Internet, the place where it has enjoyed its greatest success. Its supporters are increasingly banned from popular social media platforms, and its institutions have a hard time raising money.

Further, *Alt-Right* is no longer a large umbrella term, containing people with many different ideological dispositions.

It is now used almost exclusively by people committed to explicit white identity politics. It has also lost its reputation as a fun movement—a place where people frustrated with so-called political correctness could safely blow off steam. Few people still view it as a group of irreverent, right-wing provocateurs, attacking "social justice warriors" with tongue-in-cheek humor.

Although the most prominent figures in the Alt-Right have spent the last year trying to take their movement into the real world, anonymous online trolls are still doing their work in the virtual world. It is not obvious whether they are presently very effective, however. The 2016 presidential election was a unique moment—an opportunity for the angry, anonymous right-wing masses to work spontaneously toward a single goal. With the election over, the online Alt-Right trolls are mostly a chaotic mess.

In the face of these challenges, the Alt-Right is turning on itself. It is presently rife with infighting. Different groups with different strategies are constantly sniping at each other. The movement furiously debates "optics," with some declaring that they need to present themselves as ordinary Trump supporters and try to work behind the scenes in the conservative movement and the Republican Party, quietly pushing the mainstream right toward white nationalism. Others insist that this amounts to capitulation, and instead argue that the movement must be as radical as possible, forever pushing the boundaries of allowable opinion. The disagreeing factions are moving in different directions and, in some cases, cutting all ties with each other.

There is no way to know which of these strategies offers the Alt-Right a better chance of a breakthrough. It is possible that neither has a chance of being particularly effective. The more important point is that the Alt-Right is further dividing, and it is not large enough to survive as a significant movement if it is splintering into feuding camps.

By pointing out the Alt-Right's present weakness, I am not suggesting that its opponents should be complacent. As we have seen, even a marginalized and weakened extreme right can be incredibly dangerous. In fact, if the Alt-Right continues to decline and its chances of achieving any real success as a conventional political movement effectively disappear, its likelihood of spawning more violent groups may increase. It is easy to imagine new groups analogous to The Order appearing on the scene. Extreme-right, lone-wolf attacks are also a significant threat, and very difficult to predict and prevent.

When thinking about the Alt-Right, however, it is important to put it into context. It is a small movement, and as its tactics become better known and its opponents become better organized, its ability to project size and strength continues to weaken. Rather than becoming a permanent fixture of American political life, the Alt-Right may be remembered as just one more oddity of the Trump era, ultimately signifying very little.

Even if the Alt-Right disappears entirely, it is still worth studying. The radical right will probably always exist, with or without the *Alt-Right* label. Its next iteration will study this current period, noting its strengths and weaknesses, and seek to do better next time.

# NOTES

## Chapter 1

1. "Richard Bertrand Spencer," Southern Poverty Law Center, accessed November 26, 2017, https://www.splcenter.org/fighting-hate/extremist-files/individual/richard-bertrand-spencer-0.

2. "The Sharon Statement: A Timeless Declaration of Conservative Principles," Young Americans for Freedom, accessed November 27, 2017, http://www.yaf.org/news/the-sharon-statement/.

3. Russell Kirk, *The Politics of Prudence*, 2nd ed. (Wilmington, DE: ISI Books, 2004), 15–29.

4. "Port Huron Statement (June 15, 1962)," Students for a Democratic Society, accessed November 27, 2017, https://history.hanover.edu/courses/excerpts/111huron.html.

5. Vox Day, "What the Alternative Right Is," *Vox Popoli*, August 24, 2016, accessed November 27, 2017, https://voxday.blogspot.com/2016/08/what-alt-right-is.html.

6. Damon T. Berry, *Blood and Faith: Christianity in American White Nationalism* (Syracuse, NY: Syracuse University Press, 2017), 3.

7. "Anti-Semitism," the Anti-Defamation League (ADL), accessed March 4, 2018, https://www.adl.org/anti-semitism.

8. John Daniszewski, "Writing About the 'Alt-Right,'" Associated Press, November 28, 2016, accessed November 30, 2017, https://blog.ap.org/behind-the-news/writing-about-the-alt-right.

9. Paul Gottfried, "A Paleo Epitaph," *Taki's Magazine*, April 7, 2008, accessed October 24, 2016, http://takimag.com/article/a_paleo_epitaph/print#axzz4O1qdT7K8.

10. Lance Williams, "White Nationalist Richard Spencer Gets His Money from Louisiana Cotton Fields—and the US Government," *Mother Jones*, March 17, 2017, accessed November 30, 2017, http://www.motherjones.com/politics/2017/03/richard-spencer-cotton-farms-louisiana-subsidies/#.

11. "Washington Post–ABC News poll Aug. 16–20, 2017," *Washington Post*, August 22, 2017, accessed February 20, 2018, https://www.washingtonpost.com/politics/polling/washington-postabc-news-poll-aug-1620/2017/08/22/f97e2352-874c-11e7-96a7-d178cf3524eb_page.html.

12. Thomas J. Main, "What's the Alt-Right, and How Large Is Its Audience?" *Los Angeles Times*, August 22, 2017, accessed November 29, 2017, http://www.latimes.com/opinion/op-ed/la-oe-main-alt-right-audience-20170822-story.html.

13. Patrick S. Forscher and Nour S. Kteily, "A Psychological Profile of the Alt-Right," Working paper.

## Chapter 2

1. Francis Parker Yockey, *Imperium: The Philosophy of History and Politics* (Sausalito, CA: Noontide Press, 1969), 508.

2. "Racist Skinhead," Southern Poverty Law Center, accessed January 13, 2018, https://www.splcenter.org/fighting-hate/extremist-files/ideology/racist-skinhead.

3. Michael Barkun, *Religion and the Racist Right: The Origins of the Christian Identity Movement* (Chapel Hill, University of North Carolina Press, 1997), 271.

4. Ibid., 228–229.

5. Jeff McKinley, "Neo-Nazi Father Is Killed; Son, 10, Steeped in Beliefs, Is Accused," *The New York Times*, May 10, 2011, accessed January 24, 2018, http://www.nytimes.com/2011/05/11/us/11nazi.html.

6. Serge F. Kovaleski, Julie Turkewitz, Joseph Goldstein, and Dan Barry, "An Alt-Right Makeover Shrouds the Swastikas," *The New York Times*, December 10, 2016, accessed January 24, 2018, https://www.nytimes.com/2016/12/10/us/alt-right-national-socialist-movement-white-supremacy.html.

7. Robert S. Griffin, *The Fame of a Dead Man's Deeds: An Up-Close Portrait of White Nationalist William Pierce* (Self-Published, 2001), 105.

8. Elaine Frantz Parsons, "Midnight Rangers: Costume and Performance in the Reconstruction-Era Ku Klux Klan," *Journal of American History*, 92(2005): 811–836.

9. Keegan Hankes, "Dylann Roof May Have Been a Regular Commenter at Neo-Nazi Website Daily Stormer," Southern Poverty Law Center, June 21, 2015, accessed December 28, 2017, https://www.splcenter.org/hatewatch/2015/06/21/dylann-roof-may-have-been-regular-commenter-neo-nazi-website-daily-stormer.

## Chapter 3

1. Emma Grey Ellis, "How the Alt-Right Grew from an Obscure Racist Cabal," *Wired*, October 9, 2016, accessed December 4, 2017, https://www.wired.com/2016/10/alt-right-grew-obscure-racist-cabal/.

2. Naomi Wolf, "Fascist America, in Ten Easy Steps," *The Guardian*, April 24, 2007, accessed March 6, 2016, http://www.theguardian.com/world/2007/apr/24/usa.comment.

3. Jonah Goldberg, *Liberal Fascism: The Secret History of the American Left from Mussolini to the Politics of Change* (New York: Crown Forum, 2009).

4. Roger Griffin, *Modernism and Fascism: The Sense of a Beginning Under Mussolini and Hitler* (New York: Palgrave Macmillan, 2007), 181.

5. Dylan Matthews, "I Asked 5 Fascism Experts Whether Donald Trump Is a Fascist. Here's What They Said," *Vox*, December 10, 2015, accessed March 6, 2016, http://www.vox.com/policy-and-politics/2015/12/10/9886152/donald-trump-fascism.

6. "Fascism Today: An Interview with Shane Burley," *Revolution by the Book: The AK Press Blog*, December 27, 2017, accessed January 5, 2018, http://www.revolutionbythebook.akpress.org/fascism-today-an-interview-with-shane-burley/.

7. J. Lester Feder and Pierre Buet, "The Man Who Gave White Nationalism a New Life," *Buzzfeed*, December 26, 2017, accessed January 7, 2018, https://www.buzzfeed.com/lesterfeder/the-man-who-gave-white-nationalism-a-new-life?utm_term=nrV7zBoPp#.sseL9z7pZ.

8. Eric Westervelt, "How Russia Weaponized Social Media with 'Social Bots,'" *National Public Radio*, November 5, 2017, accessed

March 28, 2018, https://www.npr.org/2017/11/05/562058208/
how-russia-weaponized-social-media-with-social-bots.

9. "The Alt-Right Uprising: Who's Really Pulling the Puppet
Strings?" *The Glenn Beck Program*, March 2, 2018, accessed
March 28, 2018, http://www.glennbeck.com/2018/03/02/
the-alt-right-uprising-and-whos-really-pulling-the-puppet-
strings/.

10. Ben Collins and Joseph Cox, "Jenna Abrams, Russia's Clown
Troll Princess, Duped the Mainstream Media and the World," *The
Daily Beast*, November 2, 2017, accessed March 28, 2018, https://
www.thedailybeast.com/jenna-abrams-russias-clown-troll-
princess-duped-the-mainstream-media-and-the-world.

**Chapter 4**

1. Cas Mudde, "The Populist Zeitgeist," *Government and Opposition*,
39(2004), 543.

2. Ben Stanley, "The Thin Ideology of Populism," *Journal of Political
Ideologies*, 13(2008): 95–110.

3. For a refutation of the claim that populism can be properly
classified as an ideology in any sense, see Paris Aslanidis, "Is
Populism an Ideology? A Refutation and a New Perspective,"
*Political Studies*, October 2015, 88–104.

4. Margaret Canovan, "Trust the People! Populism and the Two
Faces of Democracy," *Political Studies*, 47(1999): 3.

5. Michael P. Federici, *The Challenge of Populism: The Rise of Right-
Wing Democratism in Post-War America* (New York: Praeger,
1991), 38.

6. "Patrick Joseph Buchanan, 'Culture War Speech: Address
to the Republican National Convention' (17 August 1992),"
*Voices of Democracy*, accessed December 17, 2017, http://
voicesofdemocracy.umd.edu/buchanan-culture-war-speech-
speech-text/.

7. For example, see John Ganz, "Libertarians Have More in
Common with the Alt-Right than They Want You to Think,"
*Washington Post*, September 19, 2017, accessed March 18, 2018,
https://www.washingtonpost.com/news/posteverything/wp/
2017/09/19/libertarians-have-more-in-common-with-the-alt-
right-than-they-want-you-to-think/?utm_term=.849eaafed2a4.

8. Hans-Hermann Hoppe, "Libertarianism, the Alt-Right, and
Antifa," *The Unz Review*, October 20, 2017, accessed January 25,

2018, http://www.unz.com/article/libertarianism-the-alt-right-and-Antifa/?highlight=Hoppe.

## Chapter 5

1. Fernando Alfonso III, "#EndFathersDay is the Work of 4chan, Not Feminists," *The Daily Dot*, June 13, 2014, accessed December 13, 2017, https://www.dailydot.com/irl/4chan-end-fathers-day/.

2. Michael Edison Hayden, "It's Okay to Be White: How Fox News Is Helping to Spread Neo-Nazi Propaganda," *Newsweek*, November 19, 2017, accessed January 2, 2018, http://www.newsweek.com/neo-nazi-david-duke-backed-meme-was-reported-tucker-carlson-without-context-714655.

3. "ADL Joins with 'Pepe' Creator Matt Furie in Social Media Campaign to #SavePepe," Anti-Defamation League (ADL), accessed December 31, 2017, https://www.adl.org/news/press-releases/adl-joins-with-pepe-creator-matt-furie-in-social-media-campaign-to-savepepe#.WAkCn_krLcs.

4. Aaron Mak, "The Far Right's New Toad Mascot Is a Fatter, More Racist Pepe the Frog," *Slate*, December 4, 2017, accessed December 31, 2017, http://www.slate.com/blogs/future_tense/2017/12/04/groyper_the_far_right_s_new_meme_is_a_more_racist_version_of_pepe_the_frog.html.

5. Jenna Wortham, "Founder of a Provocative Web Site Forms a New Outlet," *The New York Times*, March 13, 2011, accessed December 14, 2017, http://www.nytimes.com/2011/03/14/technology/internet/14poole.html?_r=1.

6. Cole Stryker, *Epic Win for Anonymous: How 4chan's Army Conquered the Web* (New York: Overlook Duckworth, 2011), 249–250.

7. Ibid., 232–233.

8. Charlie Warzel, "How the Alt-Right—and Paul Ryan's Challenger—Coordinate to Fight the 'Jewish Media,'" *Buzzfeed*, January 12, 2018, accessed January 24, 2018, https://www.buzzfeed.com/charliewarzel/how-the-alt-right-and-paul-ryans-challenger-coordinate-to?utm_term=.glMbmWLLL#.puNZdPNNN.

9. "The Twitter Rules," accessed December 19, 2017, https://help.twitter.com/en/rules-and-policies/twitter-rules.

10. Ashley Feinberg, "This is The Daily Stormer's Playbook," *Huffpost*, December 13, 2017, accessed January 1, 2018, https://

www.huffingtonpost.com/entry/daily-stormer-nazi-style-guide_
us_5a2ece19e4b0ce3b344492f2.

11. Colin Liddell, "Andrew Anglin's Inverted Ghetto," *Alternative Right*, September 26, 2014, accessed January 1, 2018, https://alternativeright.blog/2014/09/26/andrew-anglins-inverted-ghetto/.

12. Keegan Hankes, "Dylann Roof May Have Been a Regular Commenter at Neo-Nazi Website The Daily Stormer," Southern Poverty Law Center, July 21, 2015, accessed February 24, 2018, https://www.splcenter.org/hatewatch/2015/06/21/dylann-roof-may-have-been-regular-commenter-neo-nazi-website-daily-stormer.

13. Andrew Anglin, "First Blog Post," *Andrew Anglin*, August 24, 2017, accessed January 1, 2018, https://andrewanglinblog. wordpress.com/2017/08/24/first-blog-post/.

14. Luke O'Brien, "America's Most Notorious Neo-Nazi Is on the Lam. Won't You Come Home, Andrew Anglin?" *Huffpost*, December 19, 2017, accessed January 2, 2018, https://www.huffingtonpost.com/entry/on-the-lam-with-andrew-anglin-americas-most-notorious-neo-nazi_us_5a33fb5ae4b01d429cc86842.

## Chapter 6

1. Aram Roston and Joel Anderson, "The Moneyman Behind the Alt-Right," *Buzzfeed*, July 23, 2017, accessed December 8, 2017, https://www.buzzfeed.com/aramroston/hes-spent-almost-20-years-funding-the-racist-right-it?utm_term=.ciVjVJzgE#. frMdwLzar.

2. "Funding Hate: How White Supremacists Raise Their Money," Ant-Defamation League, accessed December 8, 2017, https://www.adl.org/education/resources/reports/funding-hate-how-white-supremacists-raise-their-money#introduction-.

3. "25 Points," Traditionalist Worker Party, accessed January 29, 2018, https://www.tradworker.org/points/.

4. "Frequently Asked Questions," Identity Evropa, accessed January 30, 2018, https://www.identityevropa.com/faq.

5. Emma Cott, "How Our Reporter Uncovered a Lie That Propelled an Alt-Right Extremist's Rise," *The New York Times*, February 5, 2018, accessed March 4, 2019, https://www.nytimes.com/2018/02/05/insider/confronting-a-white-nationalist-eli-mosley.html.

6. "The Future of Identity Evropa," *Red Ice Radio*, December 1, 2017, accessed January 30, 2018, https://redice.tv/red-ice-radio/the-future-of-identity-evropa.

7. Ned Oliver, "James Fields of Ohio Now Facing First-Degree Murder Charge in Charlottesville Car Attack Aug. 12," *Richmond Times-Dispatch*, December 14, 2017, accessed February 24, 2018, http://www.richmond.com/news/virginia/james-fields-of-ohio-now-facing-first-degree-murder-charge/article_f1946117-c3bb-58dd-a222-38bac4f761ce.html.

8. Sam Levin, "Steve Bannon Brands Far Right 'Losers' and Contradicts Trump in Surprise Interview," *The Guardian*, August 16, 2017, accessed February 10, 2018, https://www.theguardian.com/us-news/2017/aug/17/steve-bannon-calls-far-right-losers-trump-warns-china-trade-war-american-prospect.

9. Dan Merica, "Trump Says Both Sides to Blame Amid Charlottesville Backlash," *CNN Politics*, August 16, 2017, accessed February 10, 2018, https://www.cnn.com/2017/08/15/politics/trump-charlottesville-delay/index.html.

10. Julius Krein, "I Voted for Trump. And I Sorely Regret It," *The New York Times*, August 17, 2017, accessed February 11, 2018, https://www.nytimes.com/2017/08/17/opinion/sunday/i-voted-for-trump-and-i-sorely-regret-it.html.

11. A. C. Thompson, "Police Stood by as Mayhem Mounted in Charlottesville," *ProPublica*, August 12, 2017, accessed February 11, 2018, https://www.propublica.org/article/police-stood-by-as-mayhem-mounted-in-charlottesville.

12. Vernon Freeman and Melissa Hipolit, "Charlottesville Police Chief Denies Officers Were Told Not to Intervene in Rally," *CBS 6*, August 14, 2017, accessed February 11, 2018, http://wtvr.com/2017/08/14/charlottesville-police-chief-denies-officers-were-told-not-to-intervene-in-rally/.

13. Christopher Mathias, "A Republican Running to Replace Paul Ryan Comes with White Nationalist Street Cred," *HuffPost*, December 16, 2017, accessed December 19, 2017, https://www.huffingtonpost.com/entry/paul-nehlen-white-nationalism-roy-moore-republican-party_us_5a30471de4b07ff75afe6ffd.

14. Oliver Darcy, "Bannon Adviser: Ryan Challenger Paul Nehlen Is 'Dead to Us' After Inflammatory Tweets," *CNN Money*, December 27, 2017, accessed December 31, 2017, http://money.cnn.com/

2017/12/27/media/paul-nehlen-steve-bannon-breitbart/index.
html.

15. "I'm Corey Stewart. Ask Me Anything," accessed December 19,
2017, https://www.reddit.com/r/The_Donald/comments/
615r63/im_corey_stewart_ask_me_anything/.

16. Saraya Wintersmith, "Corey Stewart Denounces KKK, Hate
Groups," *The Community Idea Station,* June 9, 2017, accessed
March 6, 2018, http://ideastations.org/radio/news/
corey-stewart-denounces-kkk-hate-groups.

**Chapter 7**

1. David Weigel and John Wagner, "Alt-Right Leader Expelled from
CPAC After Organizer Denounces 'Fascist Group,'" *Washington
Post,* February 23, 2017, accessed November 28, 2017, https://
www.washingtonpost.com/news/powerpost/wp/2017/02/23/
cpac-organizer-denounces-alt-right-as-left-wing-fascist-group/
?utm_term=.0add3d422788.

2. In Bobbio's own words: "[T]here is an element which typifies
the doctrines and movements which are called and universally
recognized as left-wing, and that is the element of egalitarianism,
by which we mean a tendency to praise that which makes people
more equal rather than that which makes people less equal."
Norberto Bobbio, *Left and Right: The Significance of Political
Distinction,* Trans. Allan Cameron (Chicago: University of
Chicago Press, 1996), 71.

3. Ramesh Ponnuru, "A Conservative No More," *National Review,*
October 11, 1999, 36.

4. "President Bush's Second Inaugural Address," *National Public
Radio,* January 20, 2005, accessed November 29, 2017, https://
www.npr.org/templates/story/story.php?storyId=4460172.

5. Richard A. Viguerie, *The New Right: We're Ready to Lead* (Falls
Church, VA: The Viguerie Company, 1980).

6. Nicole Hoplin and Ron Robinson, *Funding Brothers: The Unsung
Heroes of the Conservative Movement* (Washington, DC: Regnery,
2008), 185–210.

7. Ibid., 5.

8. George Nash, *The Conservative Intellectual Movement in America
Since 1945: 30th Anniversary Edition* (Wilmington, DE: ISI
Books, 2006).

9. Irving Kristol, *Neo-Conservatism: The Autobiography of an Idea* (New York: The Free Press, 1995), 346.

10. For the most notorious example of this, see this unsigned editorial (which was likely written by Buckley): "Why the South Must Prevail," *National Review,* 4, no. 7 (1957): 148–149.

11. Kevin P. Phillips, *The Emerging Republican Majority* (New Rochelle, NY: Arlington House, 1969), 25.

12. Derek Thompson, "Half of Fox News' Viewers Are 68 and Older," *The Atlantic,* January 27, 2014, accessed December 9, 2017, https://www.theatlantic.com/business/archive/2014/01/half-of-fox-news-viewers-are-68-and-older/283385/.

## Chapter 8

1. Jon Greenberg, "Fiorina: Trump's Abortion Flip Flop," *PolitiFact,* August 11, 2015, accessed February 22, 2016, http://www.politifact.com/truth-o-meter/statements/2015/aug/11/carly-fiorina/fiorina-trumps-abortion-flip-flop/.

2. "Donald Trump @ CPAC 2011," YouTube, accessed February 22, 2016, https://www.youtube.com/watch?v=PlT9fAkj0XU&feature=youtu.be.

3. Phil Hirschkorn, "Trump Proposes Massive One-Time Tax on the Rich," CNN.com, November 9, 1999, accessed February 23, 2016, http://www.cnn.com/ALLPOLITICS/stories/1999/11/09/trump.rich/index.html?_s=PM:ALLPOLITICS.

4. Donald J. Trump, *The America We Deserve* (Los Angeles: Renaissance Books, 2000), 169–190.

5. Niraj Chokshi, "The 100-Plus Times Donald Trump Assured Us That America Is a Laughingstock," *Washington Post,* January 27, 2016, accessed March 24, 2016, https://www.washingtonpost.com/news/the-fix/wp/2016/01/27/the-100-plus-times-donald-trump-has-assured-us-the-united-states-is-a-laughingstock/.

6. Trump, *The America We Deserve,* 145.

7. Russ Choma, "Donald Trump's Yooge Flip-Flop on Outsourcing," *Mother Jones,* March 2, 2016, accessed March 7, 2016, http://www.motherjones.com/politics/2016/03/donald-trump-outsourcing-flip-flop.

8. Donald J. Trump, *Crippled America: How to Make America Great Again* (New York: Threshold Editions, 2015), 43.

9. Trump, *The America We Deserve,* 133.

10. Jeremy Diamond, "Donald Trump's Bromance with Vladimir Putin," *CNN.com*, December 19, 2015, accessed February 26, 2016, http://www.cnn.com/2015/12/18/politics/donald-trump-vladimir-putin-bromance/.

11. Ibid.

12. Jeremy Diamond, "Trump: Let Putin Fight ISIS in Syria," *CNN. com*, September 27, 2015, accessed February 26, 2016, http://www.cnn.com/2015/09/27/politics/donald-trump-isis-syria-russia-60-minutes/.

13. Jesse Byrnes, "Trump on Bush Going into Iraq: 'They Lied,'" *The Hill*, February 13, 2016, accessed March 9, 2016, http://thehill.com/blogs/ballot-box/presidential-races/269410-trump-on-bush-going-into-iraq-they-lied.

14. Tessa Berenson, "Donald Trump Defends Torture at Republican Debate," *Time*, March 3, 2016, accessed March 7, 2016, http://time.com/4247397/donald-trump-waterboarding-torture/.

15. "Press Release: ADL Urges Donald Trump to Reconsider 'America First' in Foreign Policy Approach," Anti-Defamation League (ADL), April 28, 2016, accessed May 7, 2016, http://www.adl.org/press-center/press-releases/anti-semitism-usa/adl-urges-donald-trump-to-reconsider-america-first.html?referrer=https://www.google.com/#.Vy4awoSDFBc.

16. Trump, *The America We Deserve*, 95.

17. Trump, *Crippled America*, 111.

18. Trump, *The America We Deserve*, 144.

19. Ibid., 144–145.

20. Donald Trump, *Time to Get Tough: Make America Great Again* (Washington, DC: Regnery, 2011), 135.

21. Ibid., 135–136.

22. Nick Timiraos, "Trump's Immigration Policy Becomes More Tangled After Debate," *The Wall Street Journal*, March 4, 2016, accessed March 7, 2016, http://www.wsj.com/articles/trumps-immigration-policy-becomes-more-tangled-after-debate-1457132164.

23. Scott Greer, "Trump Campaign Rushes to Clarify Immigration Position Following Debate," *The Daily Caller*, March 4, 2016, accessed March 7, 2016, http://dailycaller.com/2016/03/04/trump-campaign-rushes-to-clarify-immigration-position-following-debate/.

24. Cooper Fleishman, "Inside the White Supremacist Alt-Right's Terrifying Election Celebration," *Mic*, November 9, 2016, accessed June 18, 2018, https://mic.com/articles/159070/alt-right-donald-trump-victory-celebration-racist-pepe-memes-anti-semitism-white-surpremacy-4chan-8chan-reddit#.M5FnHqMGr.

25. Jeremy Diamond, "Donald Trump Disavows the 'Alt-Right,'" *CNN*, November 23, 2016, accessed January 25, 2018, https://www.cnn.com/2016/11/22/politics/donald-trump-disavow-groups-new-york-times/index.html.

26. Salvador Hernandez, "Alt-Right and White Nationalist Supporters Led Tense Protests Against Trump's Airstrikes on Syria," *Buzzfeed*, April 8, 2017, accessed February 25, 2018, https://www.buzzfeed.com/salvadorhernandez/spencer-protests-trump-on-syria?utm_term=.bhgGZeZZW#.pqrGR4RRk.

27. Abby Ohlheiser and Caitlin Dewey, "Hillary Clinton's Alt-Right Speech, Annotated," *The Washington Post*, August 25, 2016, accessed March 7, 2018. https://www.washingtonpost.com/news/the-fix/wp/2016/08/25/hillary-clintons-alt-right-speech-annotated/?utm_term=.c0f2688dbf7f.

**Chapter 9**

1. Joshua Green, *Devil's Bargain: Steve Bannon, Donald Trump, and the Storming of the Presidency* (New York: Penguin Press, 2017), 90.

2. Sarah Posner, "How Donald Trump's New Campaign Chief Created an Online Haven for White Nationalists," *Mother Jones*, August 22, 2016, accessed December 5, 2017, http://www.motherjones.com/politics/2016/08/stephen-bannon-donald-trump-alt-right-breitbart-news/#.

3. Green, *Devil's Bargain*, 211–212.

4. Rosie Gray, "Who Is Steve Bannon Without *Breitbart*?" *The Atlantic*, January 9, 2018, accessed February 13, 2018, https://www.theatlantic.com/politics/archive/2018/01/steve-bannon-ousted-from-breitbart/550121/.

5. Milo Yiannopoulos, "An Establishment Conservative's Guide to the Alt-Right," *Breitbart*, March 29, 2016, accessed February 4, 2018, http://www.breitbart.com/tech/2016/03/29/an-establishment-conservatives-guide-to-the-alt-right/.

6. Joseph Bernstein, "Alt-White: How the Breitbart Machine Laundered Racist Hate," *Buzzfeed*, October 5, 2017, accessed December 5, 2017, https://www.buzzfeed.com/

josephbernstein/heres-how-breitbart-and-milo-smuggled-white-nationalism?utm_term=.ixMd6wrWP#.gqGQD9G7W.

7. Andrew Marantz, "The Alt-Right Branding War Has Torn the Movement in Two," *The New Yorker*, July 6, 2017, accessed February 13, 2018, https://www.newyorker.com/news/news-desk/the-alt-right-branding-war-has-torn-the-movement-in-two.

8. Mike Cernovich, "ALT-Right Subverted by Controlled Opposition," YouTube video, 52:58, filmed November 2016, posted November 2016, https://www.youtube.com/watch?v=vJm8wFvgwhU.

9. Paul Bazile, "The Kids Are Alt-Knights," *Proud Boy Magazine*, April 24, 2017, accessed February 14, 2018, http://officialproudboys.com/news/the-kids-are-alt-knights/.

10. Michael Kranz, "Former Infowars Staffers Filed a Formal Complaint Against Conspiracy Theorist Alex Jones Alleging Anti-Semitism, Racism, and Sexual Misconduct," *Business Insider*, February 28, 2018, accessed March 7, 2018, http://www.businessinsider.com/alex-jones-infowars-employees-complaint-about-sexual-harassment-2018-2.

11. News2Share, "Richard Spencer on 'Alt-Light': 'They're Con-Artists, They're Freaks,'" YouTube video, filmed May 2017, posted June 2017, https://www.youtube.com/watch?v=VL9rWCTmReM.

# ADDITIONAL READINGS

Abrajano, Marisa, and Zoltan Hajnal. *White Backlash*. Princeton, NJ: Princeton University Press, 2015.

Barkun, Michael. *Religion and the Racist Right: The Origins of the Christian Identity Movement*. Chapel Hill: University of North Carolina Press, 1997.

Bar-On, Tamir. *Where Have All the Fascists Gone?* New York: Routledge, 2007.

Berlet, Chip, and Matthew M. Lyons. *Right-Wing Populism in America: Too Close for Comfort*. New York: Guilford Press, 2000.

Berry, Damon T. *Blood and Faith: Christianity in American White Nationalism*. Syracuse, NY: Syracuse University Press, 2017.

Bray, Mark. *Antifa: The Anti-Fascist Handbook*. Brooklyn, NY: Melville House, 2017.

Burley, Shane. *Fascism Today: What It Is and How to End It*. Chico, CA: AK Press, 2017.

Churchill, Robert H. *To Shake Their Guns in the Tyrant's Face*. Ann Arbor: University of Michigan Press, 2009.

Coogan, Kevin. *Dreamer of the Day: Francis Parker Yockey and the Postwar Fascist International*. New York, NY: Autonomedia, 1998.

Daniels, Jessie. *Cyber Racism*. Lanham, MD: Rowman and Littlefield, 2009.

Darren Mulloy. *American Extremism*. New York: Routledge, 2008.

Federici, Michael P. *The Challenge of Populism: The Rise of Right-Wing Democratism in Post-War America*. New York: Praeger, 1991.

Green, Joshua. *The Devil's Bargain*. New York: Penguin Press, 2017.

Griffin, Roger. *Modernism and Fascism: The Sense of a Beginning Under Mussolini and Hitler*. New York: Palgrave Macmillan, 2007.

Hawley, George. *Right-Wing Critics of American Conservatism.* Lawrence: University Press of Kansas, 2016.

Hawley, George. *Making Sense of the Alt-Right.* New York: Columbia University Press, 2017.

Hemmer, Nichole. *Messengers of the Right.* Philadelphia: University of Pennsylvania Press, 2016.

Kinder, Donald. *Us Against Them.* Chicago: University of Chicago Press, 2016.

King, Richard, and David J. Leonard. *Beyond Hate: White Power and Popular Culture.* New York: Routledge, 2014.

Lindholm, Charles, and José Pedro Zúquete. *The Struggle for the World: Liberation Movements for the 21st Century.* Stanford, CA: Stanford University Press, 2010.

Main, Thomas J. *The Rise of the Alt-Right.* Washington, DC: Brookings Institution Press, 2018.

Mudde, Cas. *The Ideology of the Extreme Right.* Manchester, UK: Manchester University Press, 2013.

Nagle, Angela. *Kill All Normies.* Washington, DC: Zero Books, 2017.

Nash, George. *The Conservative Intellectual Movement in America Since 1945.* New York: Basic Books, 1976.

Picciolini, Christian. *White American Youth: My Descent in America's Most Violent Hate Movement—and How I Got Out.* New York: Hachette Books, 2017.

Sedgwick, Mark. *Against the Modern World: Traditionalism and the Secret Intellectual History of the 20th Century.* New York: Oxford University Press, 2004.

Simonelli, Frederick J. *American Fuehrer: George Lincoln Rockwell and the American Nazi Party.* Champaign: University of Illinois Press, 1999.

Simpon, Patricia Anne, and Helga Druxes, eds. *Digital Media Strategies of the Far Right in Europe and the United States.* Lanham, MD: Lexington Books, 2015.

Spiro, Jonathan Peter. *Defending the Master Race: Conservation, Eugenics, and the Legacy of Madison Grant.* Burlington: University of Vermont Press, 2008.

Stryker, Cole. *Epic Win for Anonymous: How 4chan's Army Conquered the Web.* London: Overlook Duckworth, 2011.

Tenold, Vegas. *Everything You Love Will Burn: Inside the Rebirth of American White Nationalism.* New York: Nation Books, 2018.

Tesler, Michael. *Post-Racial or Most-Racial?* Chicago: University of Chicago Press, 2016.

Valeri, Robin Maria, and Kevin Borgeson. *Skinhead History, Identity, and Culture.* New York: Routledge, 2018.

Zeskind, Leonard. *Blood and Politics: The History of the White Nationalist Movement from the Margins to the Mainstream.* New York: Farrar, Straus and Giroux, 2009.

# INDEX